Goldilocks
AND THE
Infinite Bears

Goldilocks
AND THE
Infinite Bears

A PIE COMICS COLLECTION

John McNamee

Once upon a time...

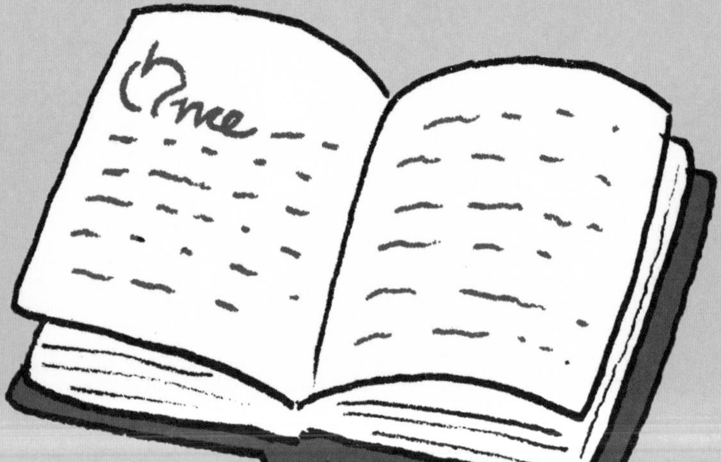
Once

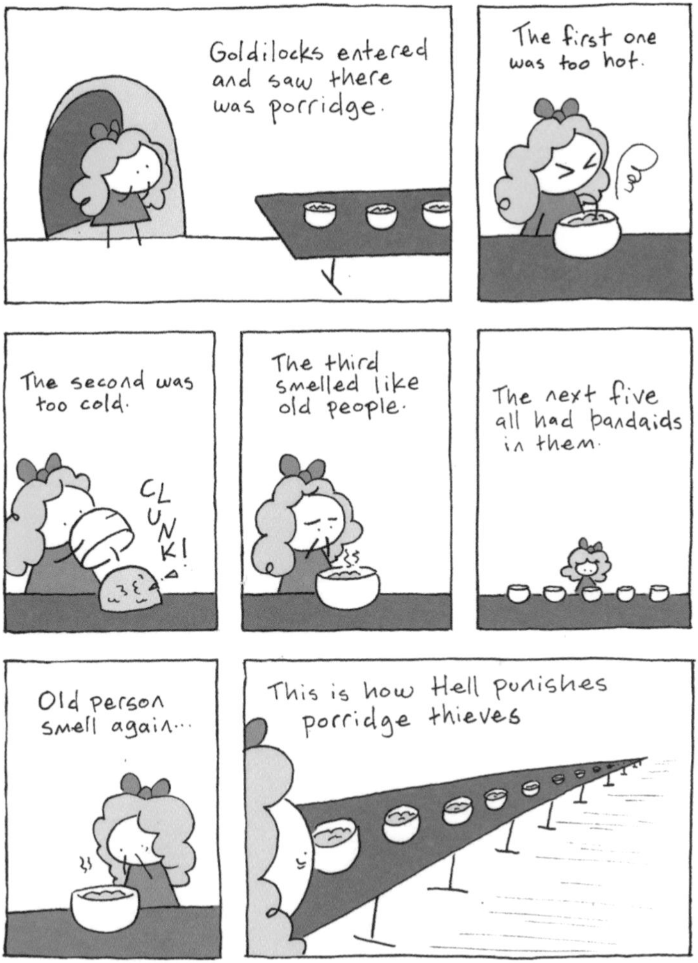
Goldilocks entered and saw there was porridge.
The first one was too hot.
The second was too cold.
CLUNK!
The third smelled like old people.
The next five all had bandaids in them.
Old person smell again...
This is how Hell punishes porridge thieves

The Frog Prince

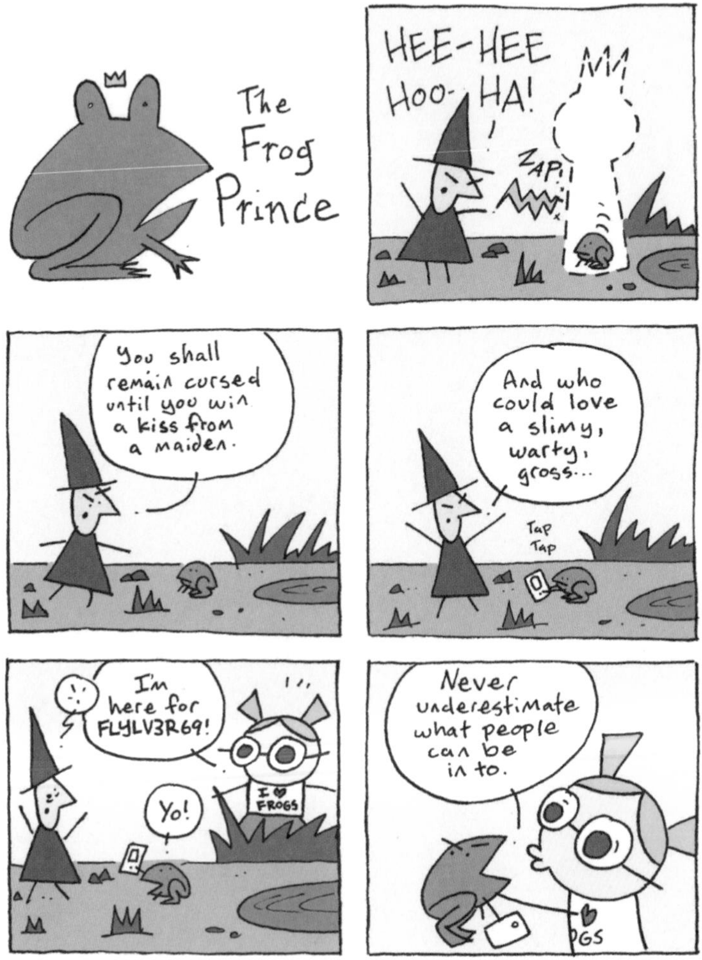
HEE-HEE HOO-HA!
ZAP!
You shall remain cursed until you win a kiss from a maiden.
And who could love a slimy, warty, gross...
Tap Tap
I'm here for FLYLV3R69!
Yo!
I ♥ FROGS
Never underestimate what people can be in to.

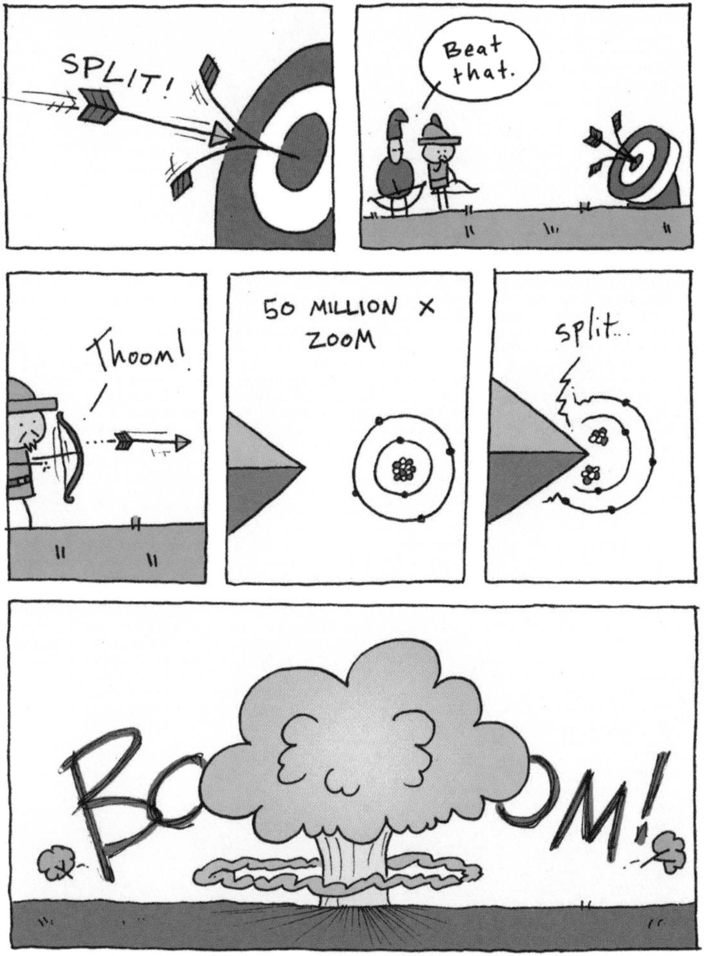
SPLIT!
Beat that.
Thoom!
50 MILLION X ZOOM
split...
BOOM!

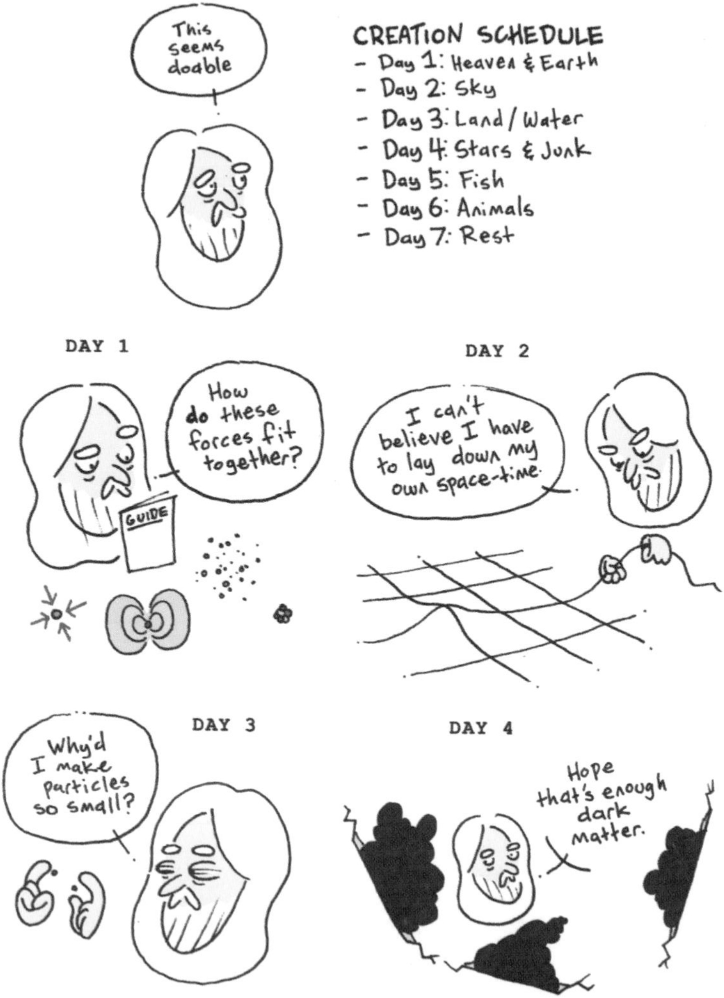
This seems doable
CREATION SCHEDULE
- Day 1: Heaven & Earth
- Day 2: Sky
- Day 3: Land / Water
- Day 4: Stars & Junk
- Day 5: Fish
- Day 6: Animals
- Day 7: Rest
DAY 1
How do these forces fit together?
GUIDE
DAY 2
I can't believe I have to lay down my own space-time.
DAY 3
Why'd I make particles so small?
DAY 4
Hope that's enough dark matter.

DAY 5

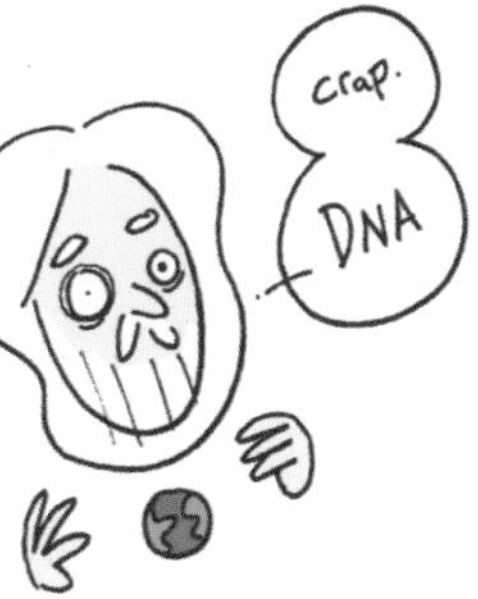
Crap.
DNA

DAY 6

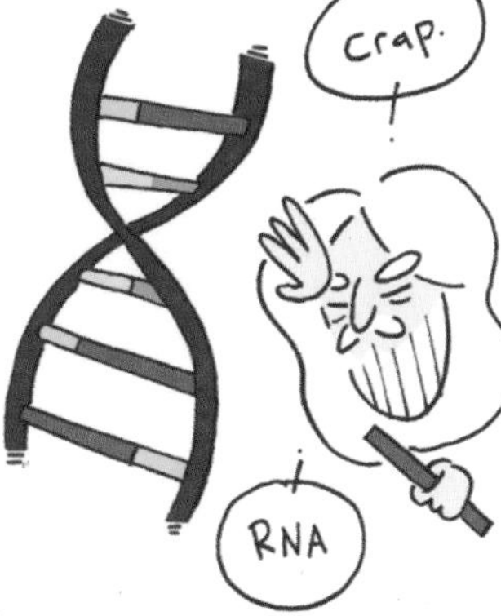
Crap.
RNA

DAY 7

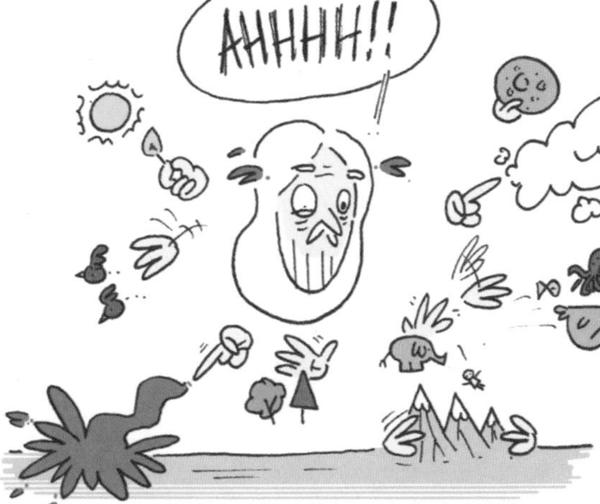
AHHHH!!

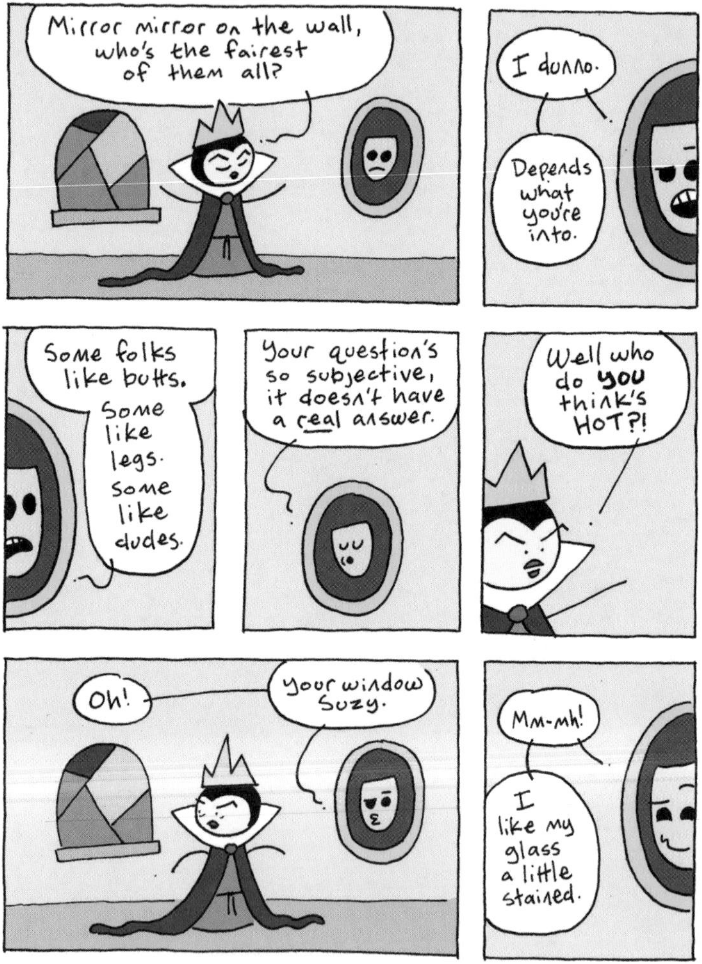
Mirror mirror on the wall, who's the fairest of them all?
I dunno.
Depends what you're into.
Some folks like butts.
Some like legs. Some like dudes.
Your question's so subjective, it doesn't have a real answer.
Well who do YOU think's HOT?!
Oh!
Your window Suzy.
Mm-mh!
I like my glass a little stained.

PEOPLE USED TO BELIEVE
THE EARTH WAS A FLAT PLATE
RESTING ON THE BACK
OF A TURTLE.

OF COURSE,
NOW WE KNOW
THAT'S SILLY.

THE EARTH
IS A SPHERE...

...BALANCED
ON THE NOSE
OF THE
CELESTIAL
SEAL.

AT THE END OF TIME,
HE'LL BE REWARDED WITH —
THE INFINITY HERRING.

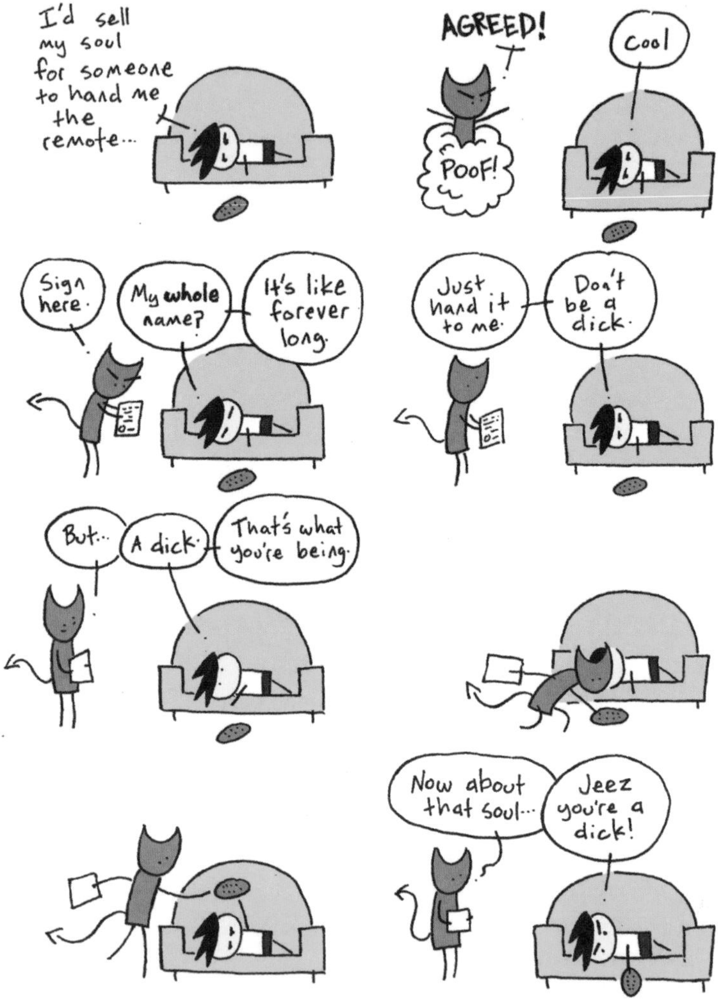
I'd sell my soul for someone to hand me the remote...
AGREED!
POOF!
Cool
Sign here.
My whole name?
It's like forever long.
Just hand it to me.
Don't be a dick.
But...
A dick.
That's what you're being.
Now about that soul...
Jeez you're a dick!

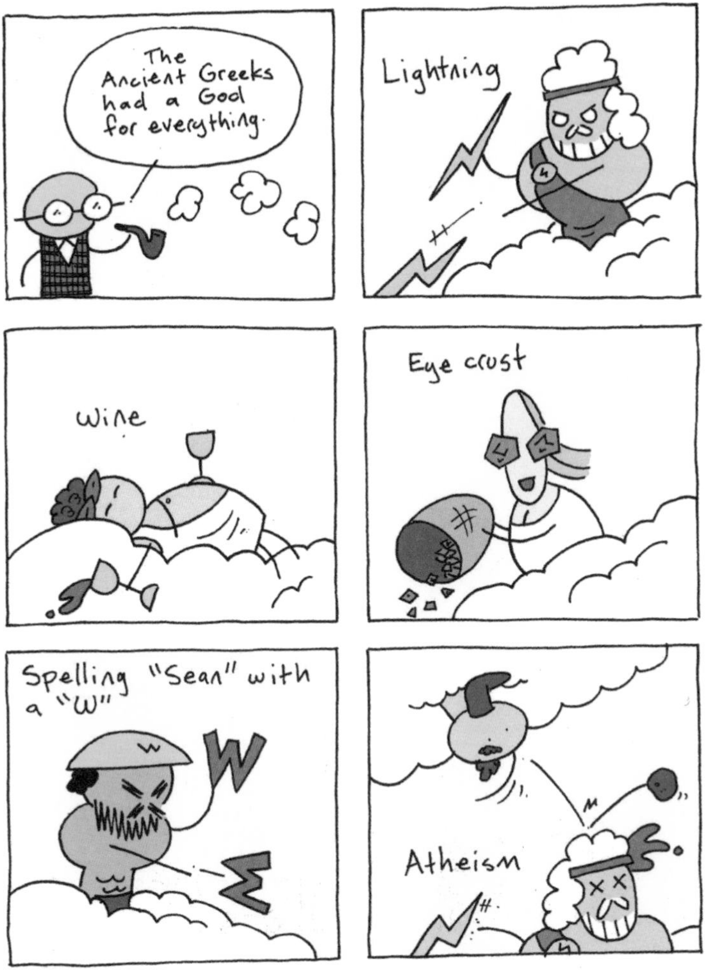
The Ancient Greeks had a God for everything.
Lightning
wine
Eye crust
Spelling "Sean" with a "W"
Atheism

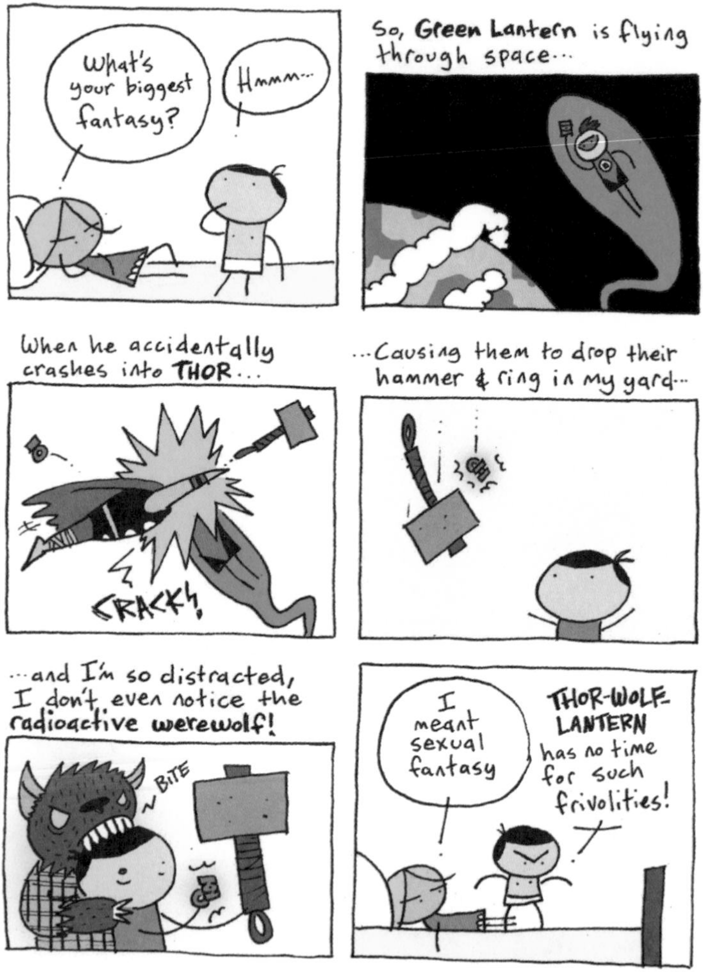
What's your biggest fantasy?
Hmmm...
So, Green Lantern is flying through space...
When he accidentally crashes into THOR...
CRACK!
...Causing them to drop their hammer & ring in my yard...
...and I'm so distracted, I don't even notice the radioactive werewolf!
BITE
I meant sexual fantasy
THOR-WOLF-LANTERN has no time for such frivolities!

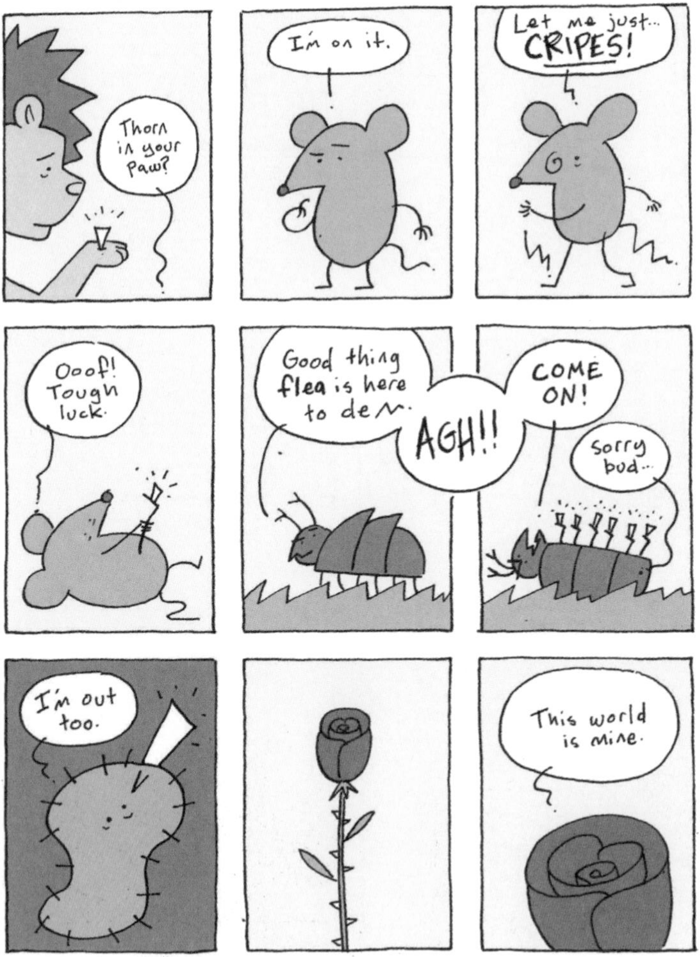
Thorn in your paw?
I'm on it.
Let me just... CRIPES!
Ooof! Tough luck.
Good thing flea is here to de
AGH!!
COME ON!
sorry bud...
I'm out too.
This world is mine.

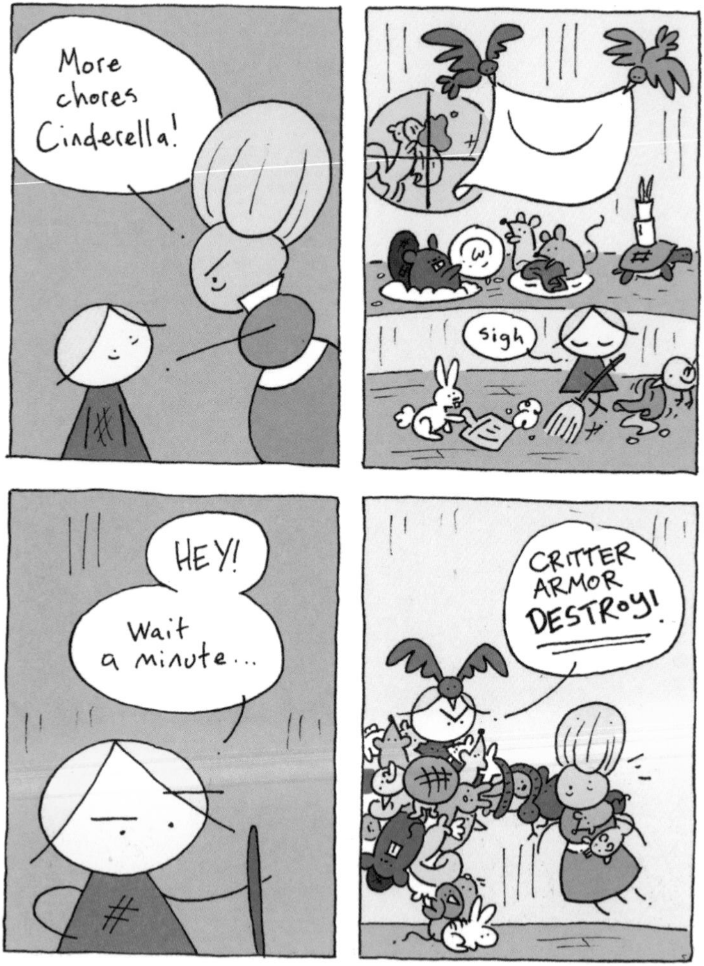
More chores Cinderella!
sigh
HEY!
Wait a minute...
CRITTER ARMOR DESTROY!

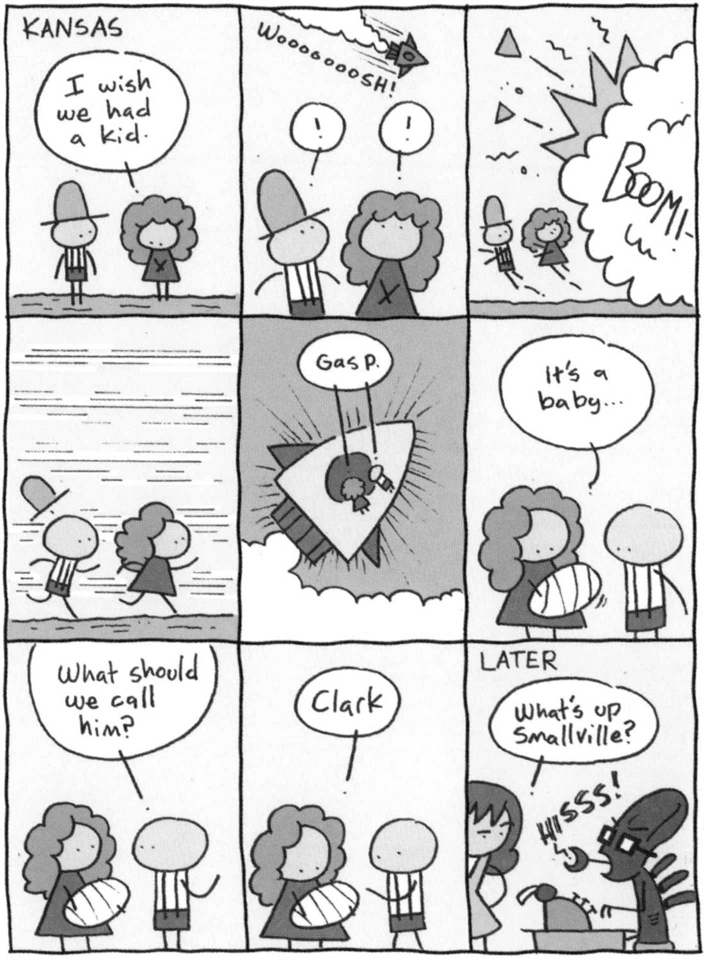
KANSAS
I wish we had a kid.
Woooooooosh!
!
!
BOOM!
Gasp.
It's a baby...
What should we call him?
Clark
LATER
What's up Smallville?
HISSS!

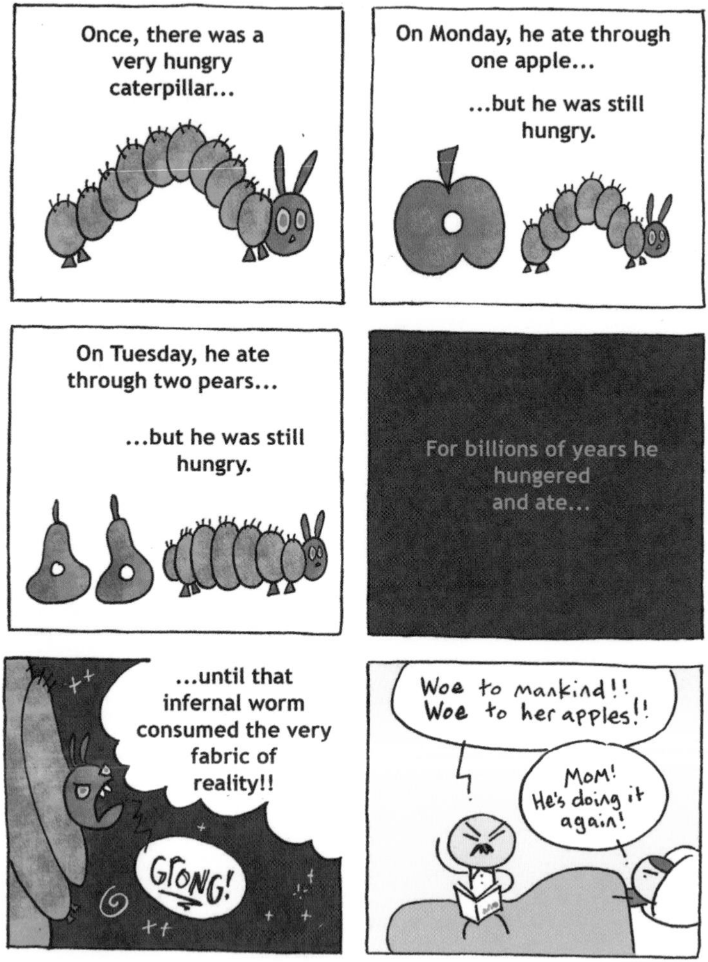

Once, there was a very hungry caterpillar...
On Monday, he ate through one apple...
...but he was still hungry.
On Tuesday, he ate through two pears...
...but he was still hungry.
For billions of years he hungered and ate...
...until that infernal worm consumed the very fabric of reality!!
GRONG!
Woe to mankind!! Woe to her apples!!
MOM! He's doing it again!

In a far away land...

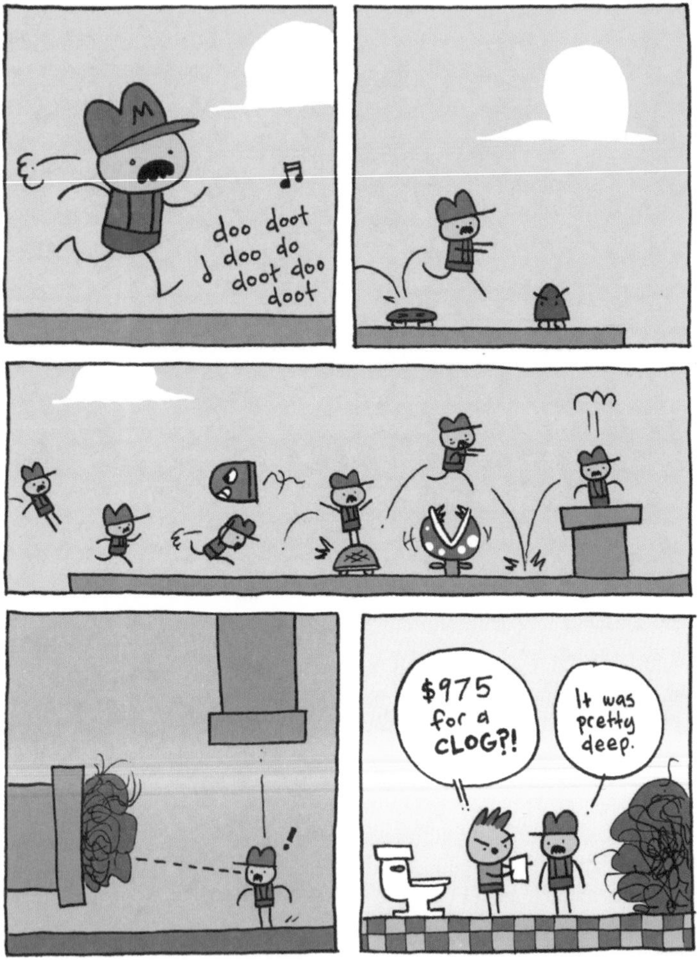
doo doot doo do doot doo doot
$975 for a CLOG?!
It was pretty deep.

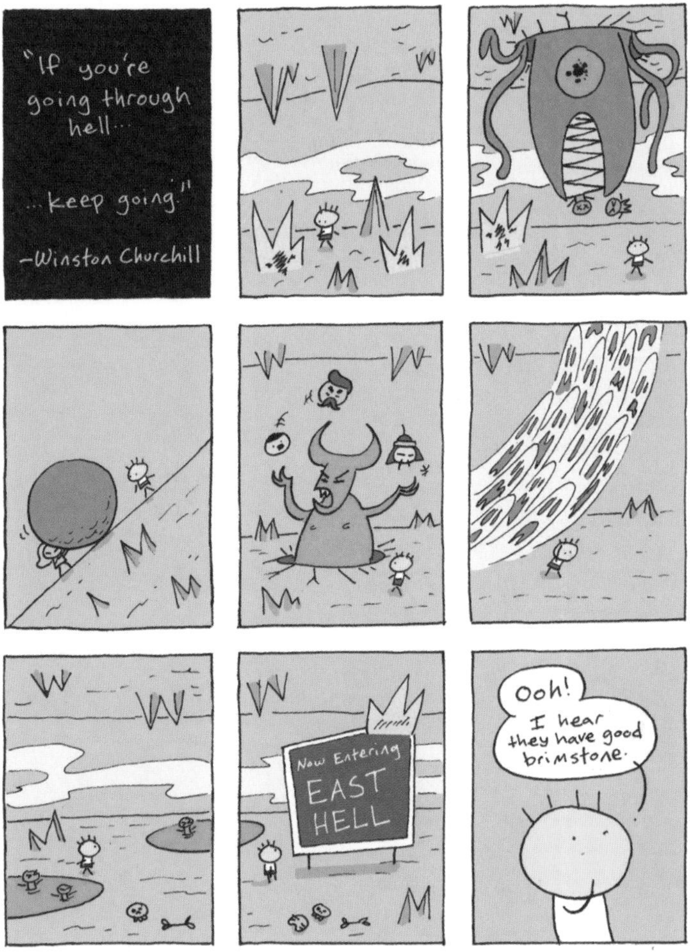
"If you're going through hell...
...keep going."
–Winston Churchill
Now Entering
EAST HELL
Ooh!
I hear they have good brimstone.

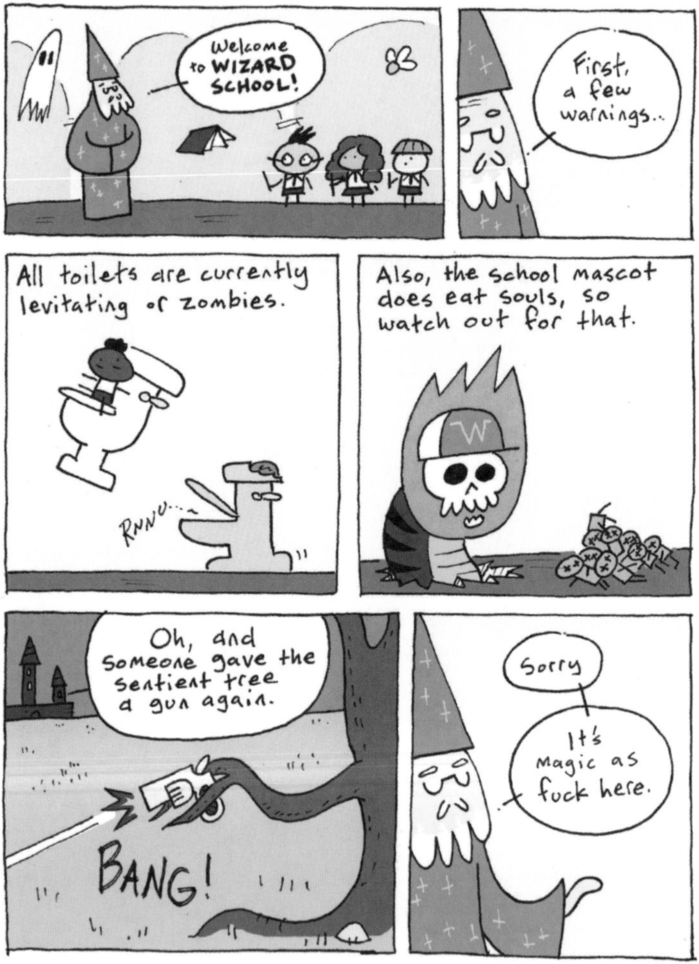
Welcome to WIZARD SCHOOL!
First, a few warnings...
All toilets are currently levitating or zombies.
RNNU...
Also, the school mascot does eat souls, so watch out for that.
Oh, and someone gave the sentient tree a gun again.
BANG!
Sorry
It's magic as fuck here.

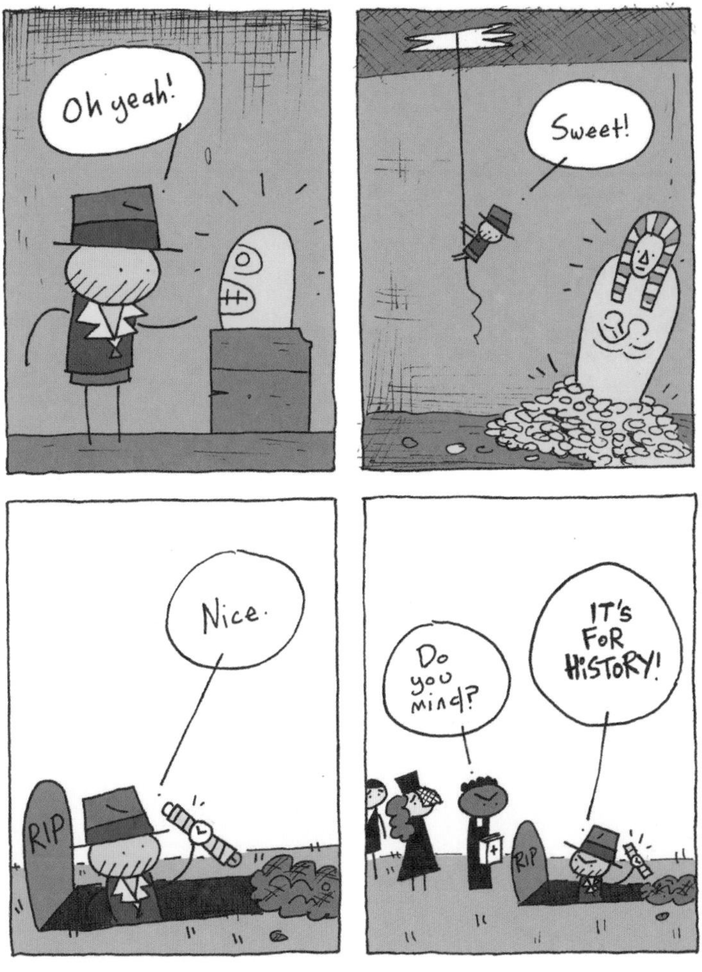
Oh yeah!
Sweet!
Nice.
Do you mind?
IT'S FOR HISTORY!
RIP
RIP

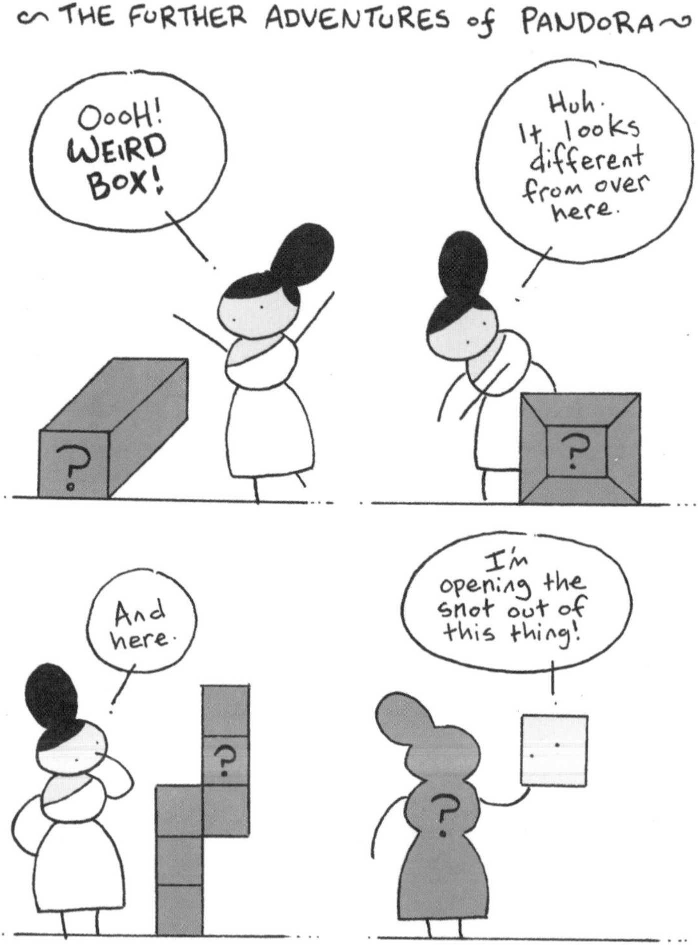
~ THE FURTHER ADVENTURES of PANDORA ~
OooH! WEIRD BOX!
Huh. It looks different from over here.
And here.
I'm opening the snot out of this thing!

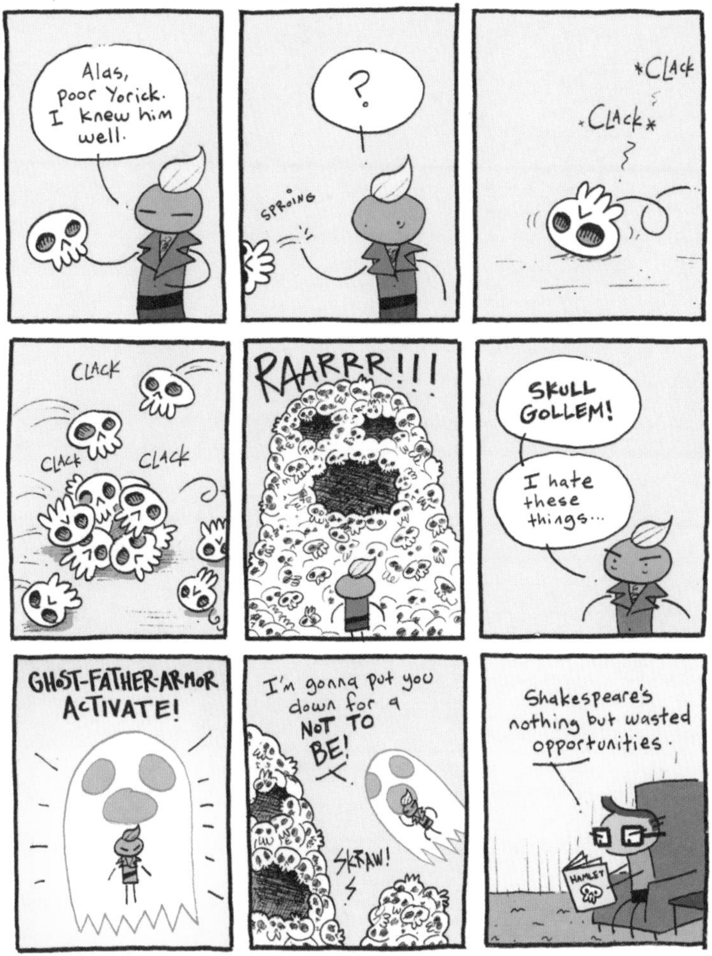
Alas, poor Yorick. I knew him well.
?
SPROING
*CLACK
CLACK
CLACK
CLACK
CLACK
RAARRR!!!
SKULL GOLLEM!
I hate these things...
GHOST-FATHER-ARMOR ACTIVATE!
I'm gonna put you down for a NOT TO BE!
SKRAW!
Shakespeare's nothing but wasted opportunities.
HAMLET

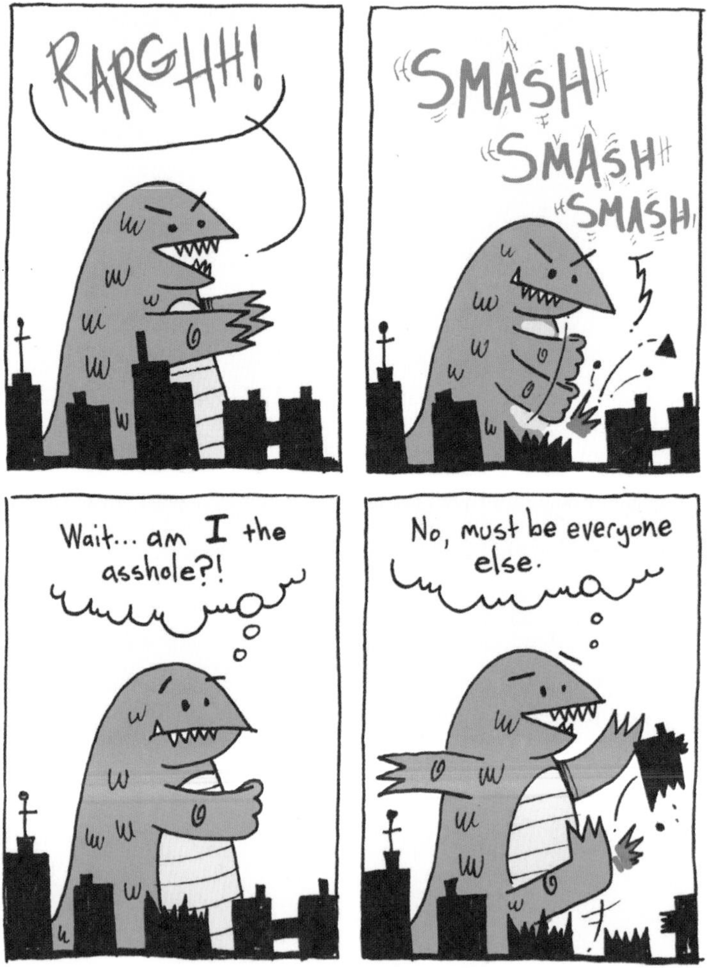
RARGHH!
SMASH
SMASH
SMASH
Wait... am I the asshole?!
No, must be everyone else.

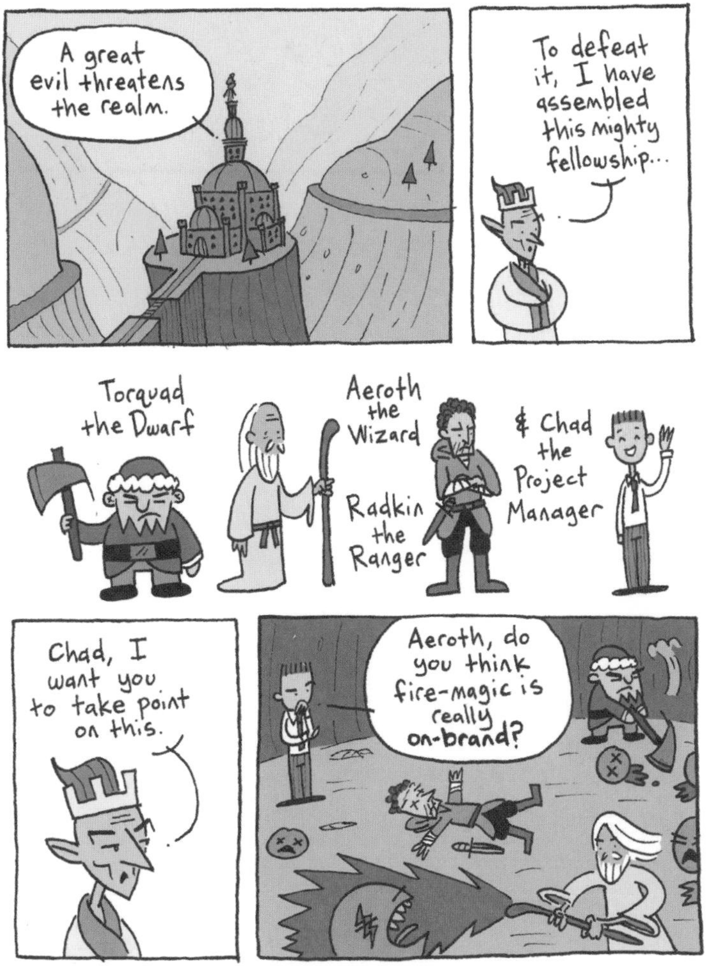
A great evil threatens the realm.
To defeat it, I have assembled this mighty fellowship...
Torquad the Dwarf
Aeroth the Wizard
Radkin the Ranger
& Chad the Project Manager
Chad, I want you to take point on this.
Aeroth, do you think fire-magic is really on-brand?

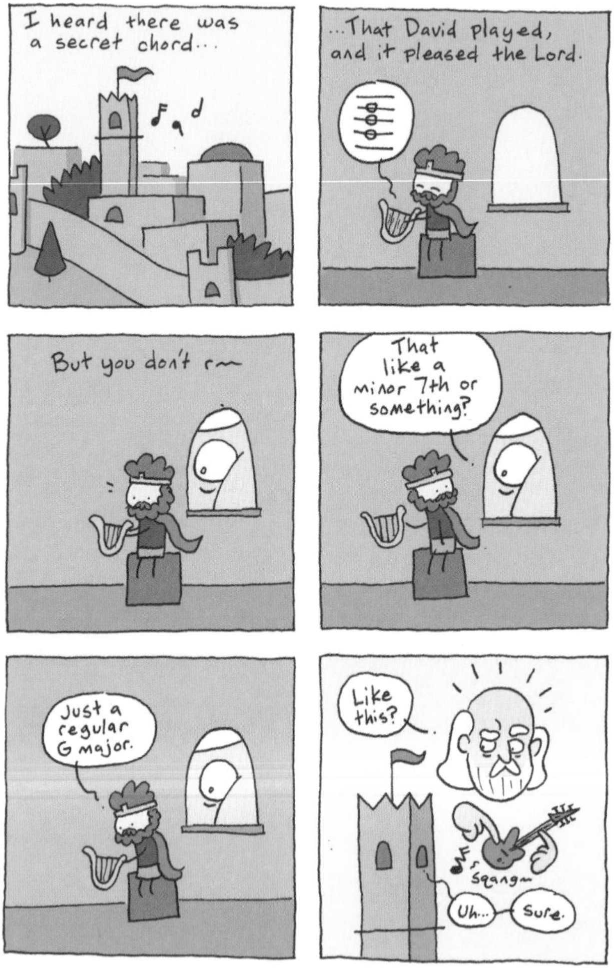
I heard there was a secret chord...
...That David played, and it pleased the Lord.
But you don't r~
That like a minor 7th or something?
Just a regular G major.
Like this?
Sqang~
Uh...
Sure.

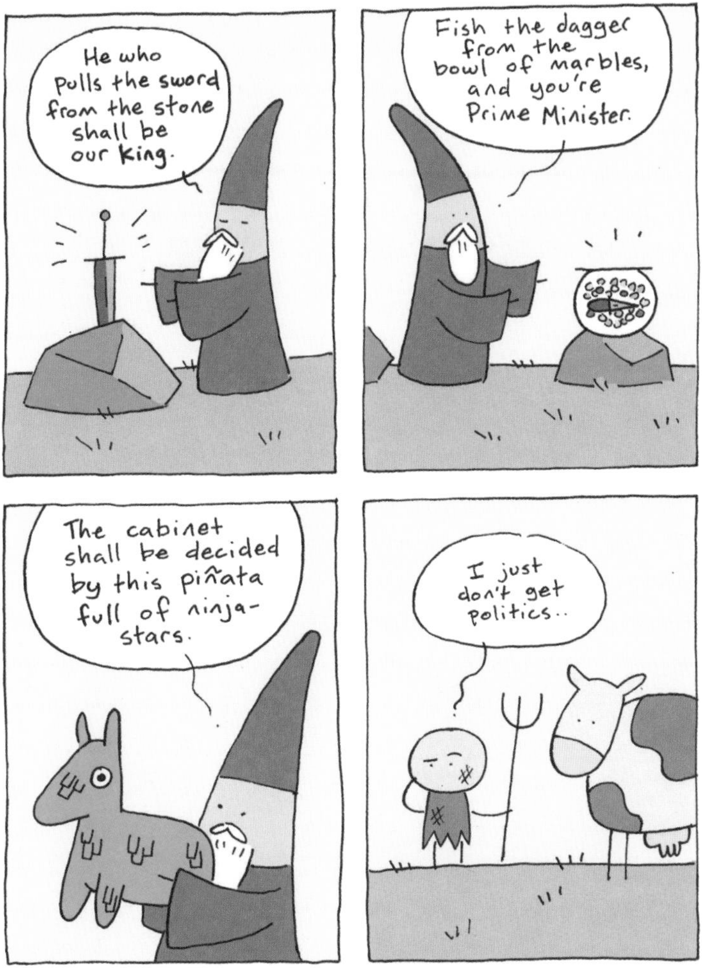
He who pulls the sword from the stone shall be our King.
Fish the dagger from the bowl of marbles, and you're Prime Minister.
The cabinet shall be decided by this piñata full of ninja-stars.
I just don't get politics..

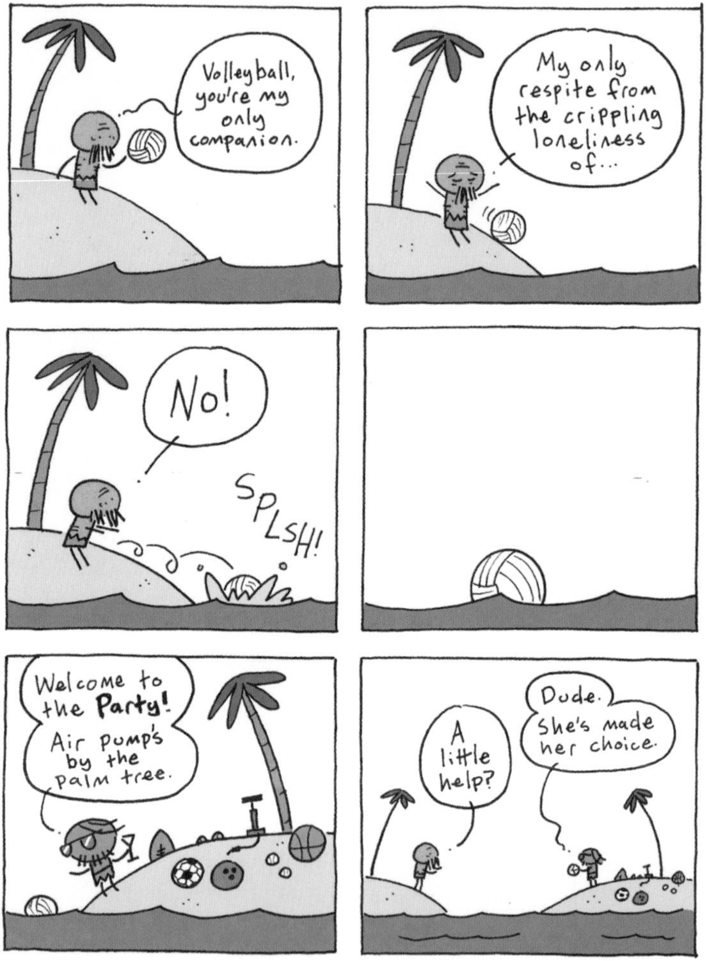

Volleyball, you're my only companion.
My only respite from the crippling loneliness of...
No!
SPLSH!
Welcome to the Party! Air pump's by the palm tree.
A little help?
Dude. She's made her choice.

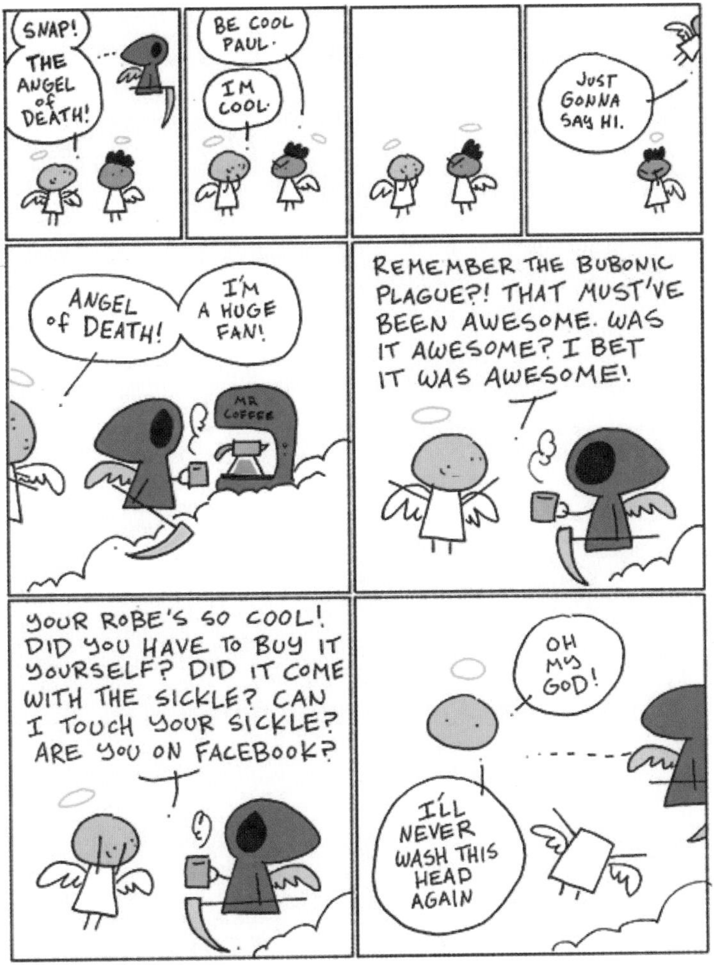
SNAP!
THE ANGEL of DEATH!
BE COOL PAUL.
IM COOL.
JUST GONNA SAY HI.
ANGEL of DEATH!
I'M A HUGE FAN!
MR COFFEE
REMEMBER THE BUBONIC PLAGUE?! THAT MUST'VE BEEN AWESOME. WAS IT AWESOME? I BET IT WAS AWESOME!
YOUR ROBE'S SO COOL! DID YOU HAVE TO BUY IT YOURSELF? DID IT COME WITH THE SICKLE? CAN I TOUCH YOUR SICKLE? ARE YOU ON FACEBOOK?
OH MY GOD!
I'LL NEVER WASH THIS HEAD AGAIN

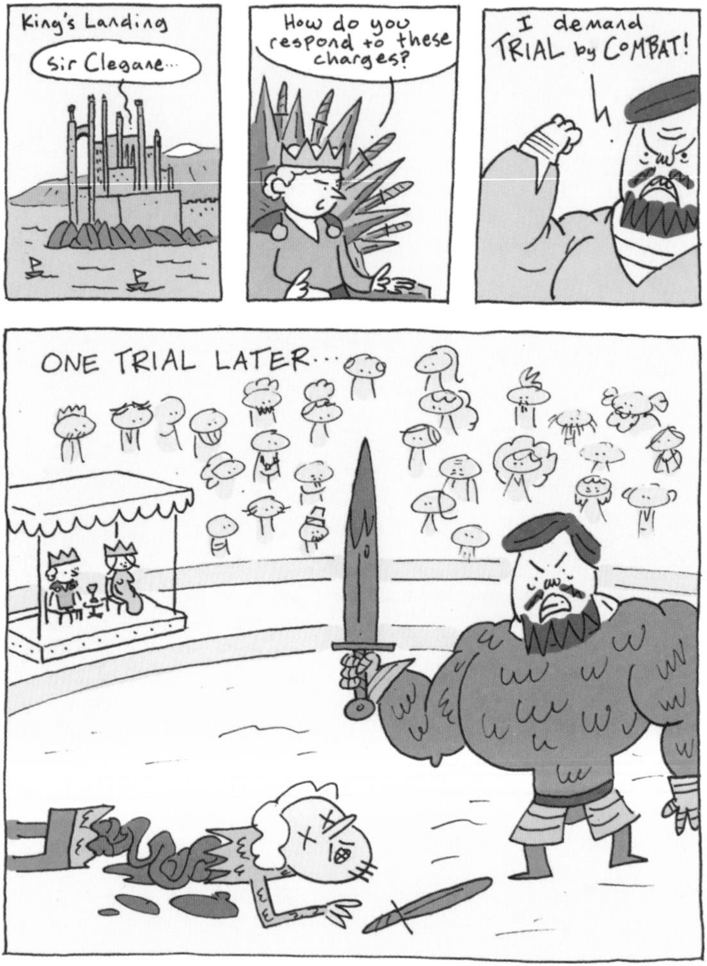
King's Landing
Sir Clegane...
How do you respond to these charges?
I demand TRIAL by COMBAT!
ONE TRIAL LATER...

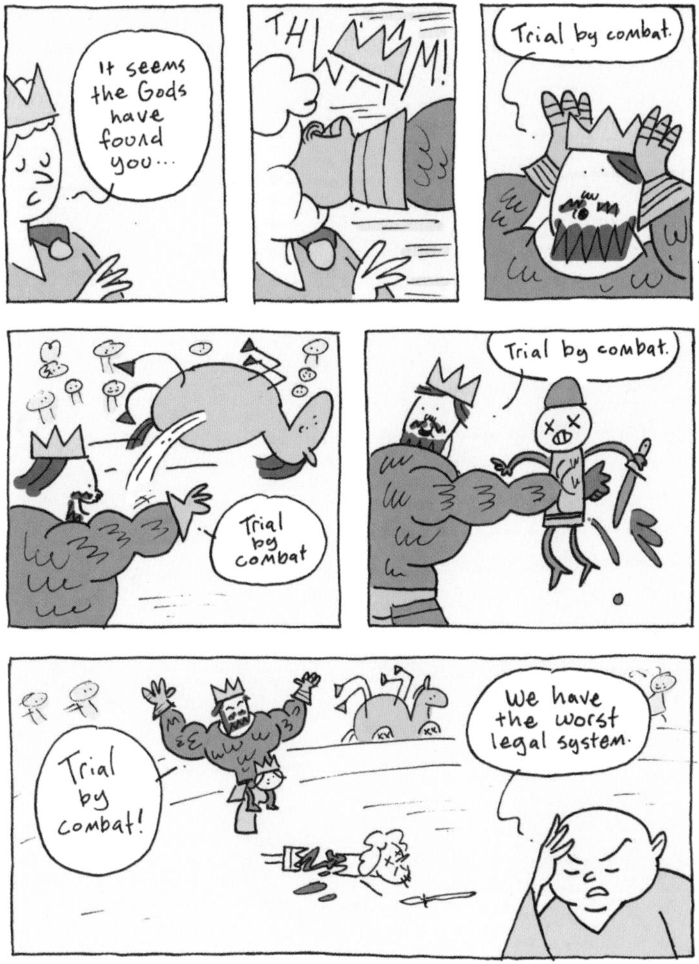
It seems the Gods have found you...
THWAM!
Trial by combat.
Trial by combat
Trial by combat.
Trial by combat!
We have the worst legal system.

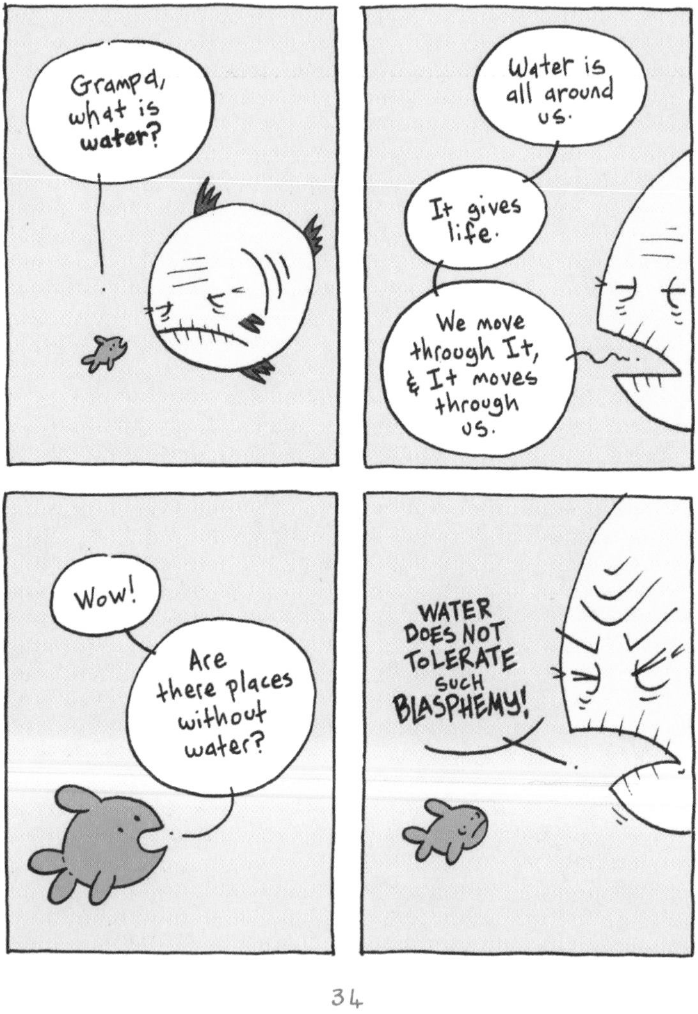
Grampa, what is **water?**
Water is all around us.
It gives life.
We move through It, & It moves through us.
Wow!
Are there places without water?
WATER DOES NOT TOLERATE SUCH BLASPHEMY!

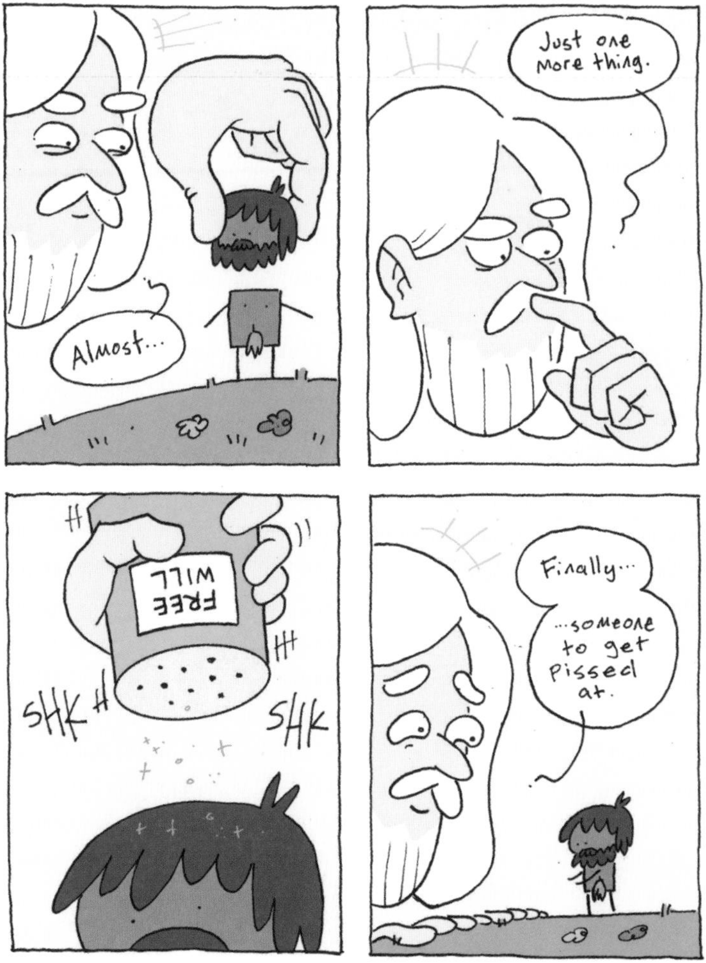
Almost...
Just one more thing.
FREE WILL
SHK
SHK
Finally...
...someone to get pissed at.

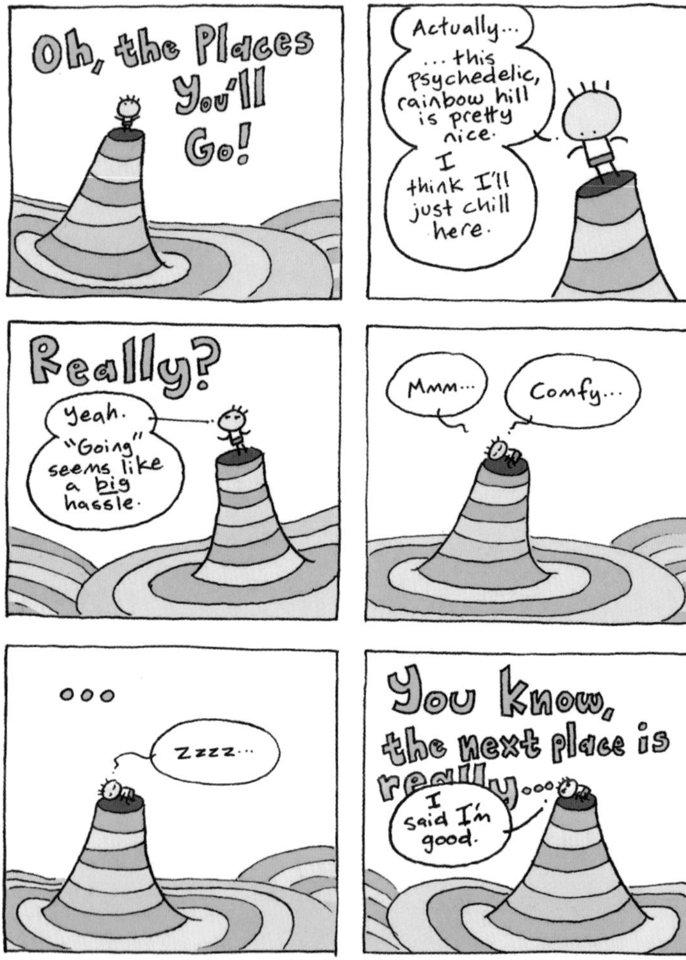
Oh, the Places You'll Go!
Actually... ...this psychedelic, rainbow hill is pretty nice. I think I'll just chill here.
Really?
Yeah. "Going" seems like a big hassle.
Mmm...
Comfy...
ooo
zzzz...
You know, the next place is really...
I said I'm good.

There lived a...

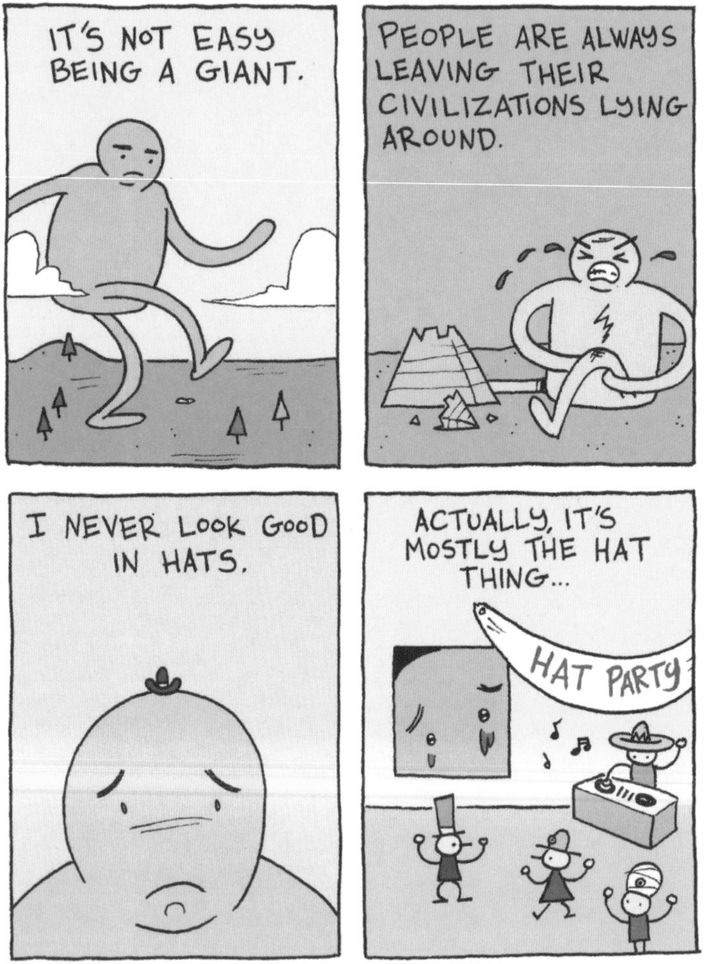
IT'S NOT EASY BEING A GIANT.
PEOPLE ARE ALWAYS LEAVING THEIR CIVILIZATIONS LYING AROUND.
I NEVER LOOK GOOD IN HATS.
ACTUALLY, IT'S MOSTLY THE HAT THING...
HAT PARTY

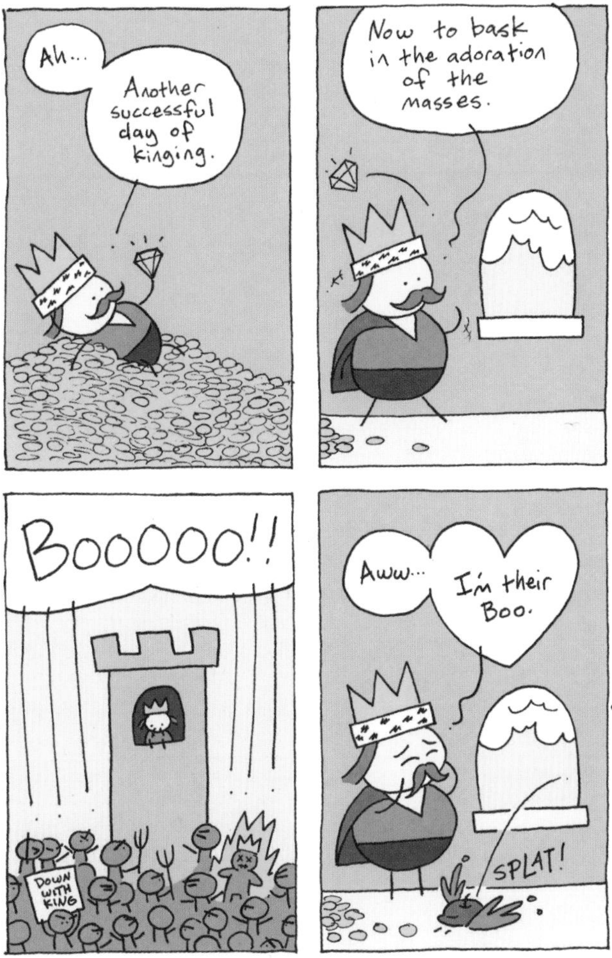
Ah...
Another successful day of kinging.
Now to bask in the adoration of the masses.
BooOOO!!
DOWN WITH KING
Aww...
I'm their Boo.
SPLAT!

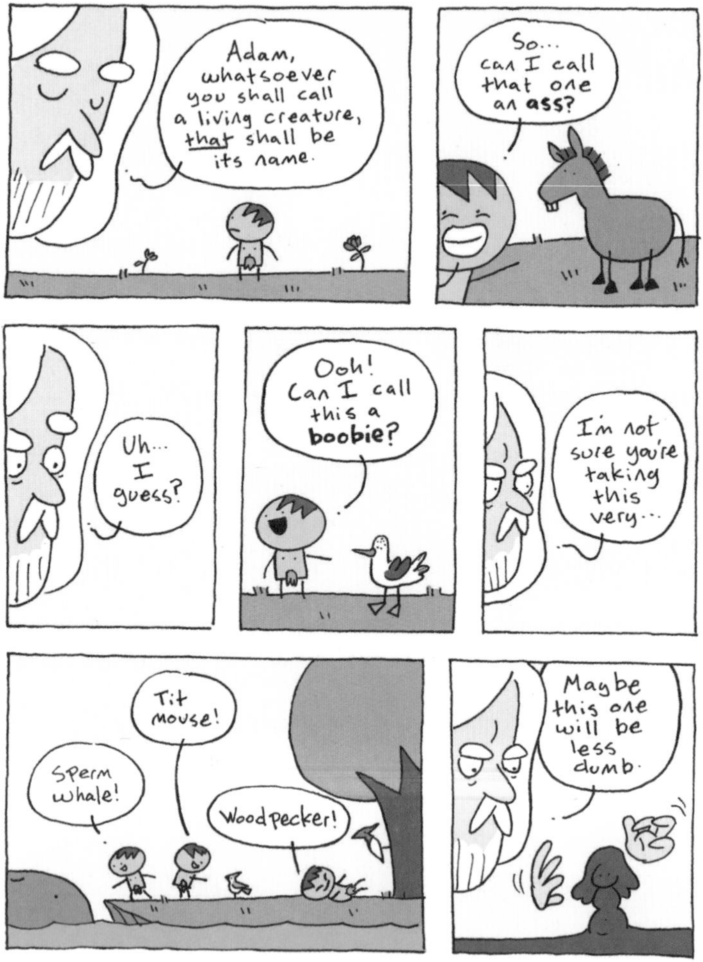
Adam, whatsoever you shall call a living creature, that shall be its name.
So... can I call that one an ass?
Uh... I guess?
Ooh! Can I call this a boobie?
I'm not sure you're taking this very...
Tit mouse!
Sperm whale!
Woodpecker!
Maybe this one will be less dumb.

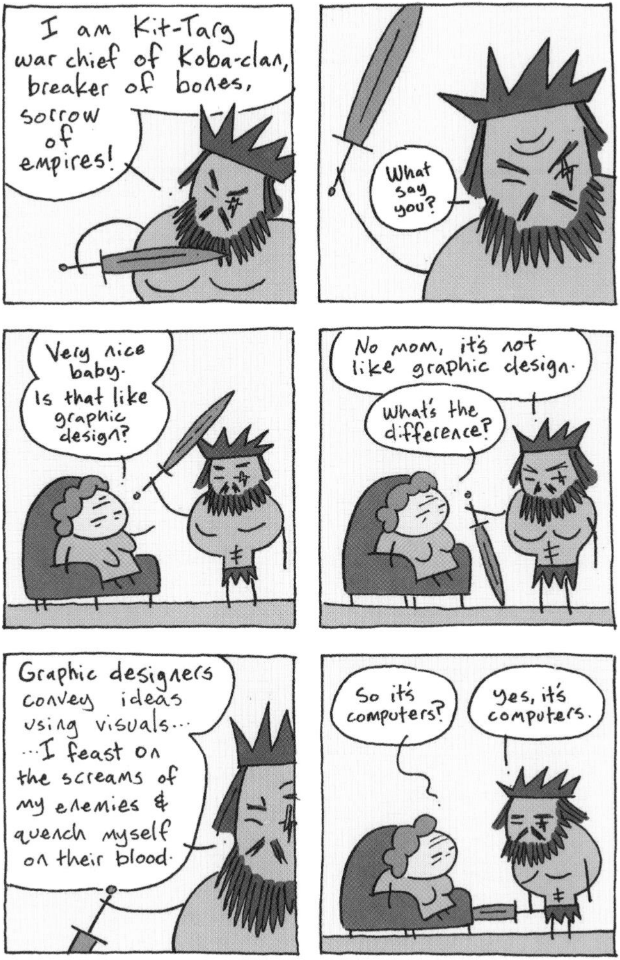
I am Kit-Targ war chief of Koba-clan, breaker of bones,
sorrow of empires!
What say you?
Very nice baby.
Is that like graphic design?
No mom, it's not like graphic design.
What's the difference?
Graphic designers convey ideas using visuals...
...I feast on the screams of my enemies & quench myself on their blood.
So it's computers?
Yes, it's computers.

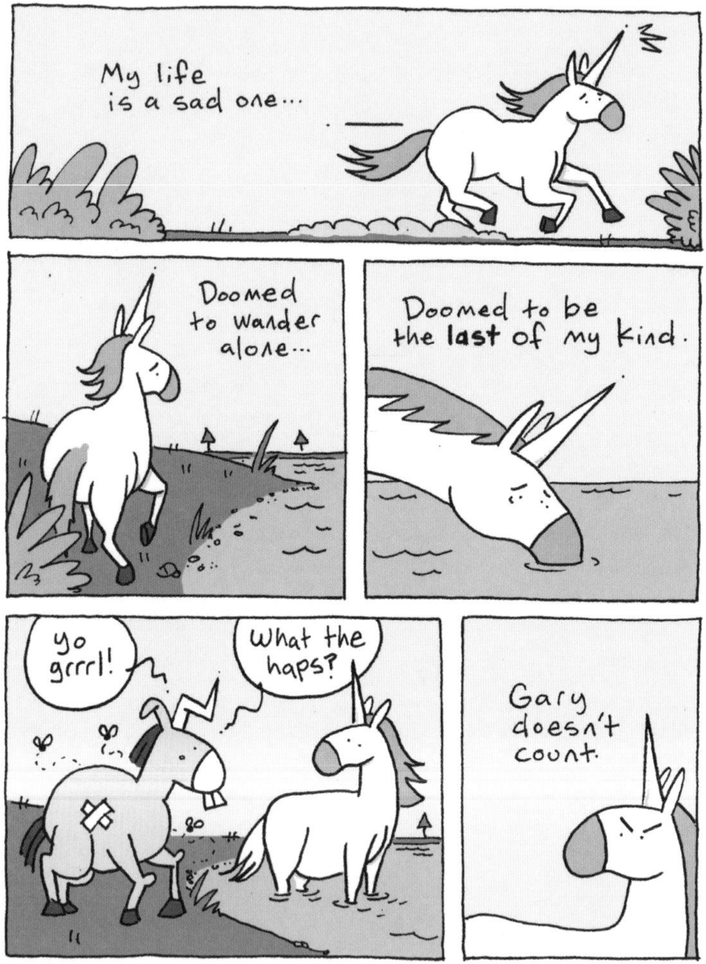
My life is a sad one...
Doomed to wander alone...
Doomed to be the **last** of my kind.
yo grrrl!
What the haps?
Gary doesn't count.

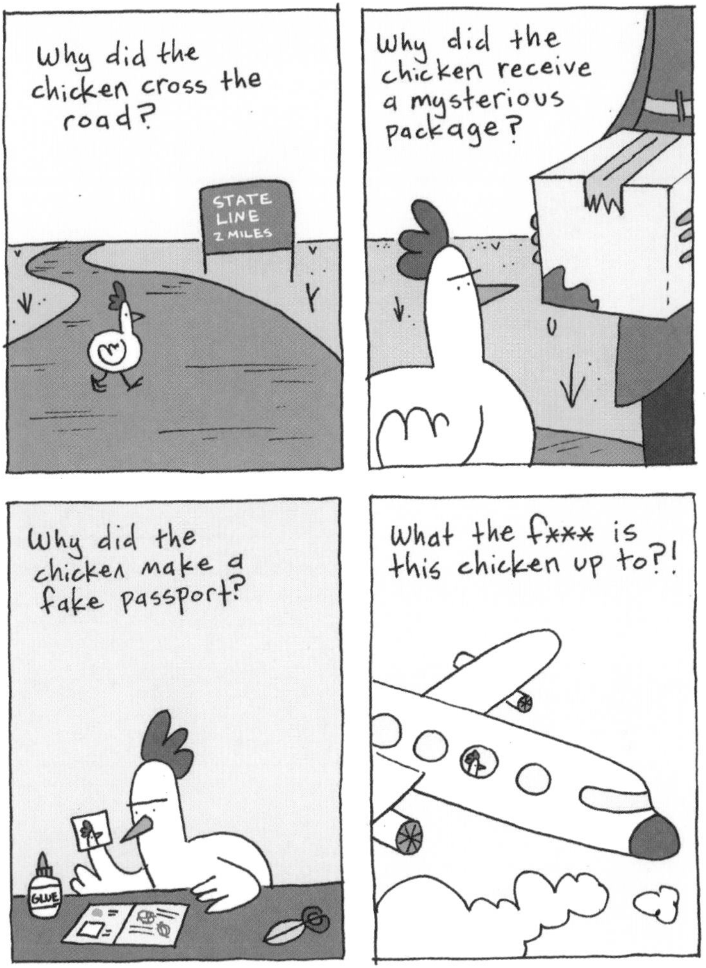
Why did the chicken cross the road?
STATE LINE 2 MILES
Why did the chicken receive a mysterious package?
Why did the chicken make a fake passport?
GLUE
What the f*** is this chicken up to?!

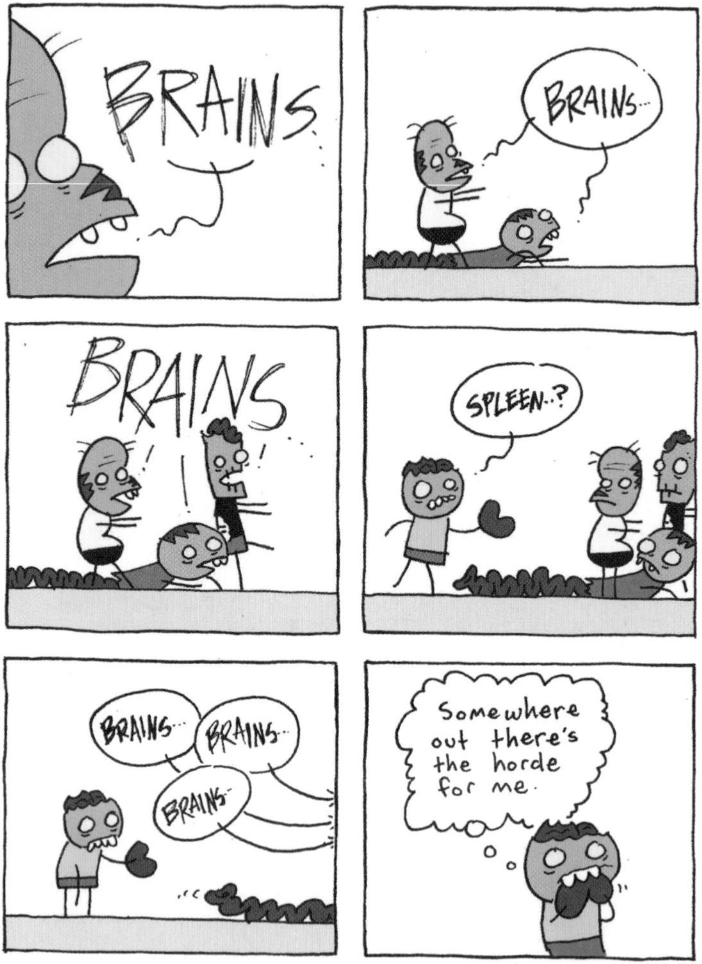
BRAINS
BRAINS...
BRAINS
SPLEEN..?
BRAINS...
BRAINS...
BRAINS
Somewhere out there's the horde for me.

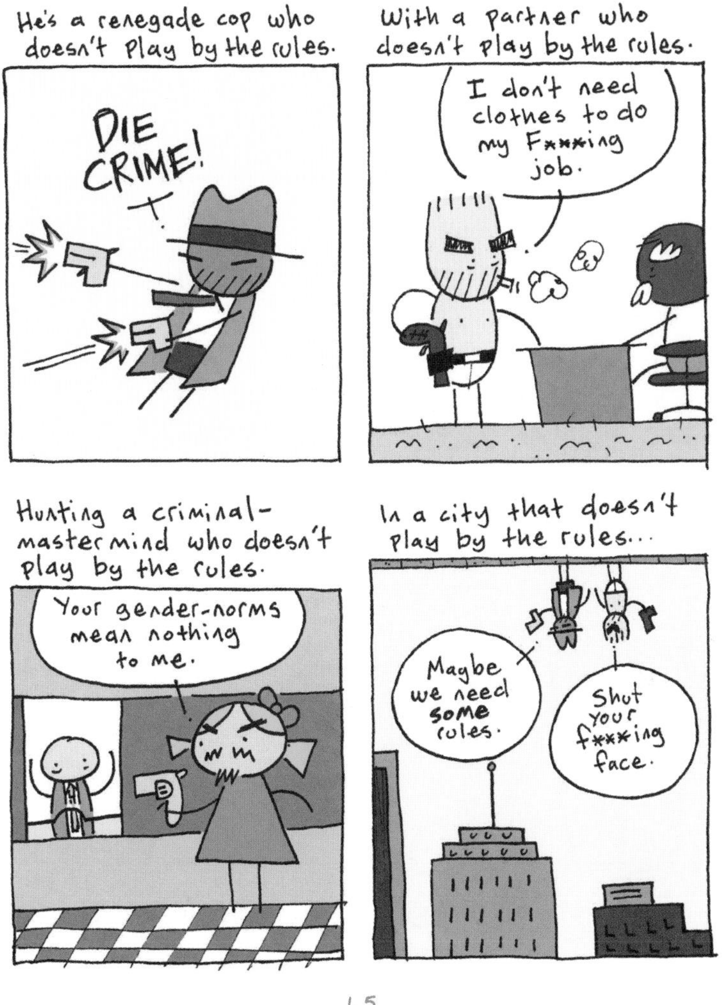
He's a renegade cop who doesn't play by the rules.
DIE CRIME!
With a partner who doesn't play by the rules.
I don't need clothes to do my F***ing job.
Hunting a criminal-mastermind who doesn't play by the rules.
Your gender-norms mean nothing to me.
In a city that doesn't play by the rules...
Maybe we need **some** rules.
Shut your f***ing face.

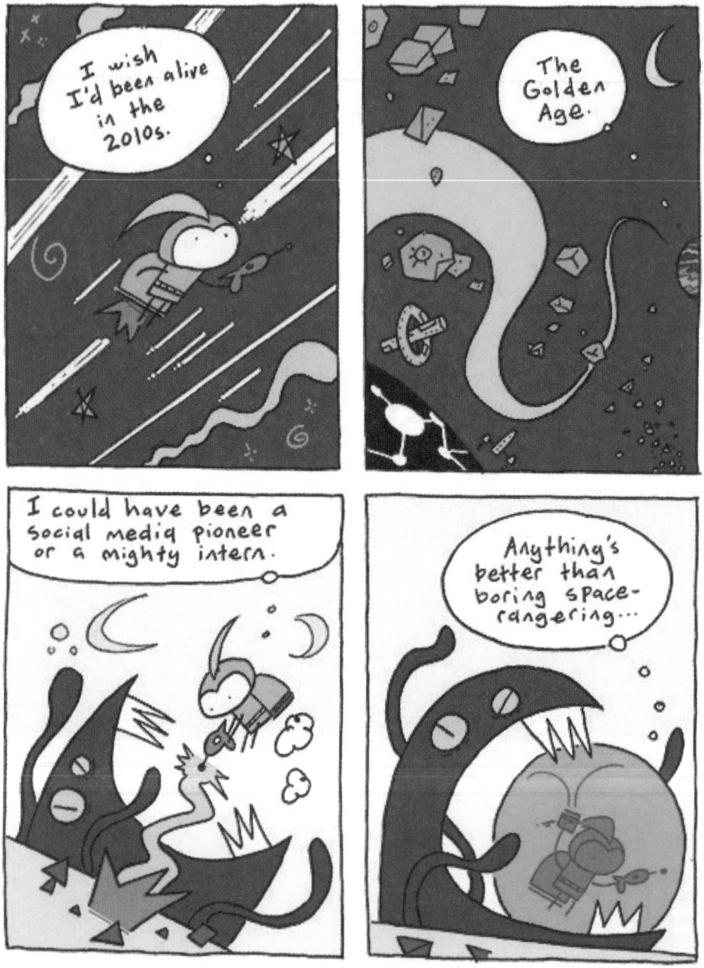
I wish I'd been alive in the 2010s.
The Golden Age.
I could have been a social media pioneer or a mighty intern.
Anything's better than boring space-rangering...

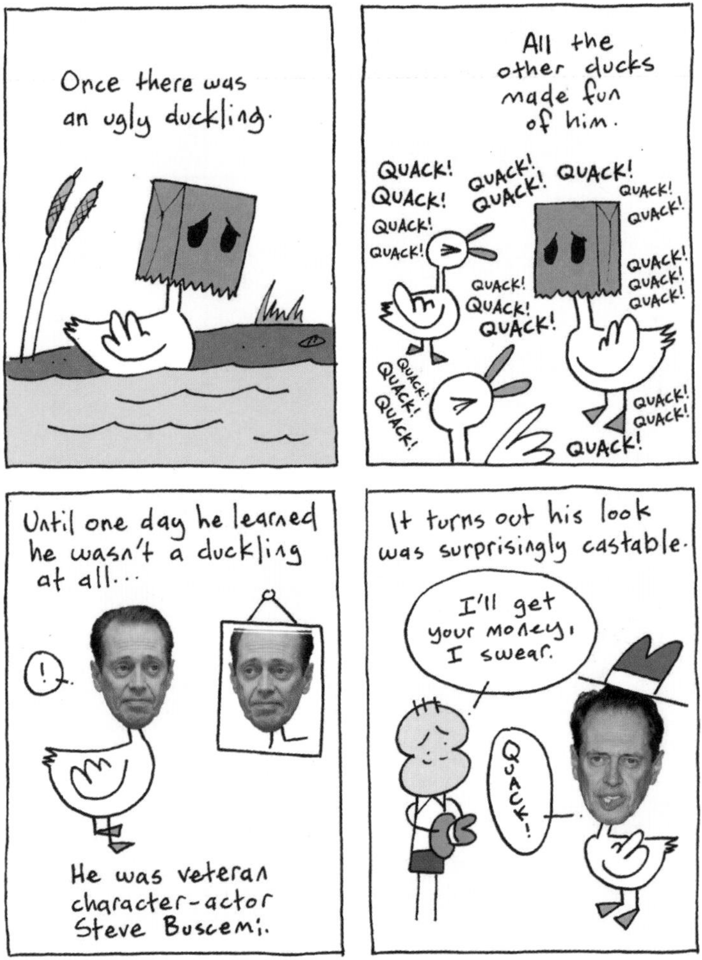
Once there was an ugly duckling.
All the other ducks made fun of him.
QUACK! QUACK! QUACK! QUACK!
QUACK! QUACK! QUACK!
QUACK! QUACK!
QUACK! QUACK! QUACK!
QUACK! QUACK! QUACK!
QUACK! QUACK! QUACK!
QUACK! QUACK! QUACK!
Until one day he learned he wasn't a duckling at all...
!
He was veteran character-actor Steve Buscemi.
It turns out his look was surprisingly castable.
I'll get your money, I swear.
QUACK!

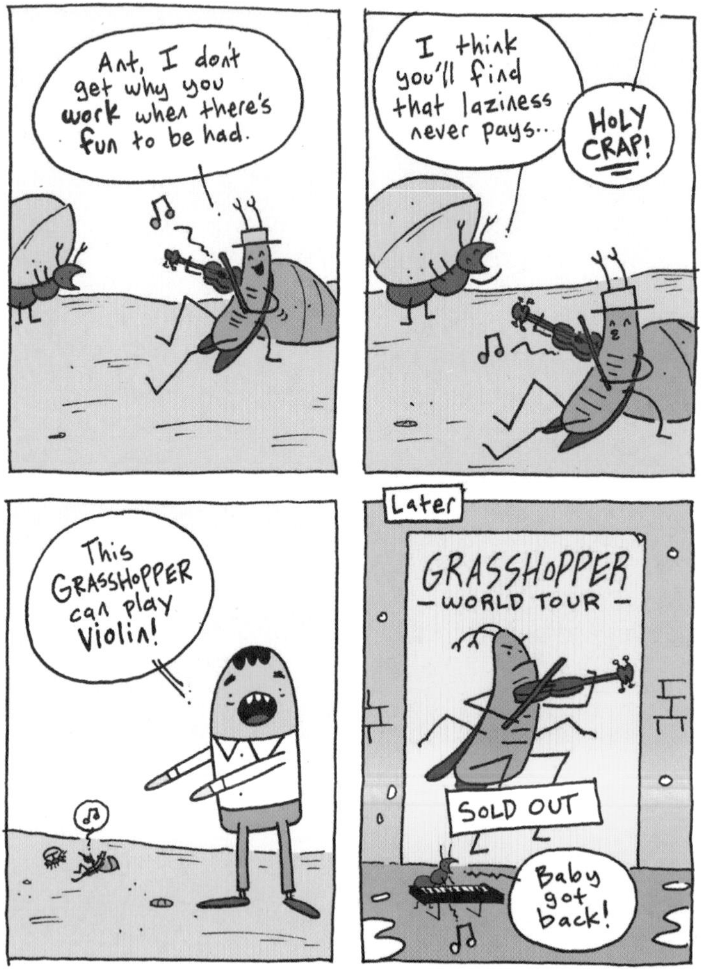
Ant, I don't get why you work when there's fun to be had.
I think you'll find that laziness never pays..
HOLY CRAP!
This GRASSHOPPER can play Violin!
Later
GRASSHOPPER
— WORLD TOUR —
SOLD OUT
Baby got back!

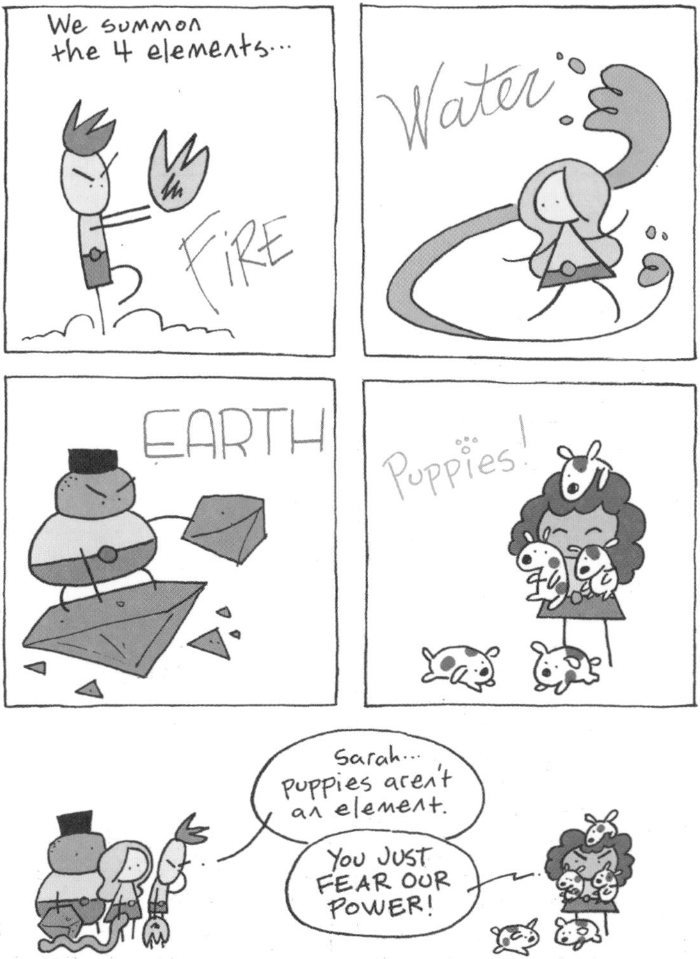
We summon the 4 elements...
FIRE
Water
EARTH
Puppies!
Sarah... puppies aren't an element.
You JUST FEAR OUR POWER!

Being a centaur is the best.
No way. Minotaur is where it's at!
I'm just glad I'm not a Jerry.
Oh yeah. Jerry's are the worst.
F*@† you guys.

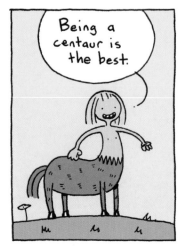

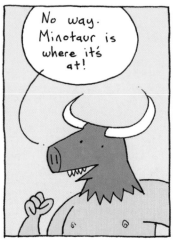

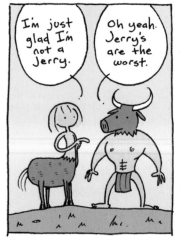

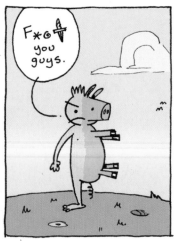

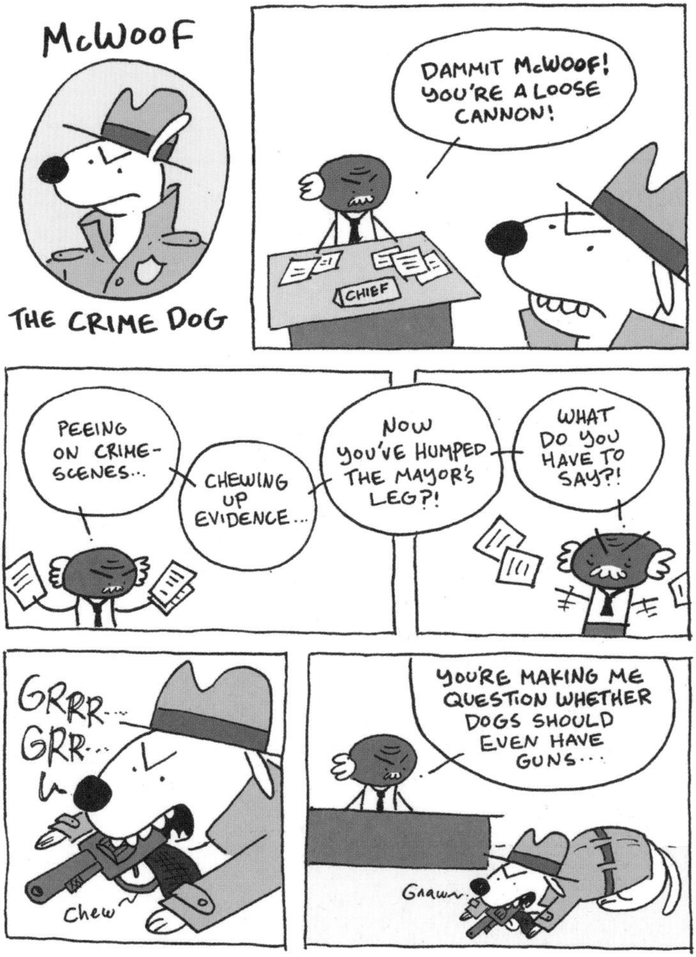
McWOOF
THE CRIME DOG
DAMMIT McWOOF! YOU'RE A LOOSE CANNON!
CHIEF
PEEING ON CRIME-SCENES...
CHEWING UP EVIDENCE...
NOW YOU'VE HUMPED THE MAYOR'S LEG?!
WHAT DO YOU HAVE TO SAY?!
GRRR... GRR... u
Chew
YOU'RE MAKING ME QUESTION WHETHER DOGS SHOULD EVEN HAVE GUNS...
Gnaw

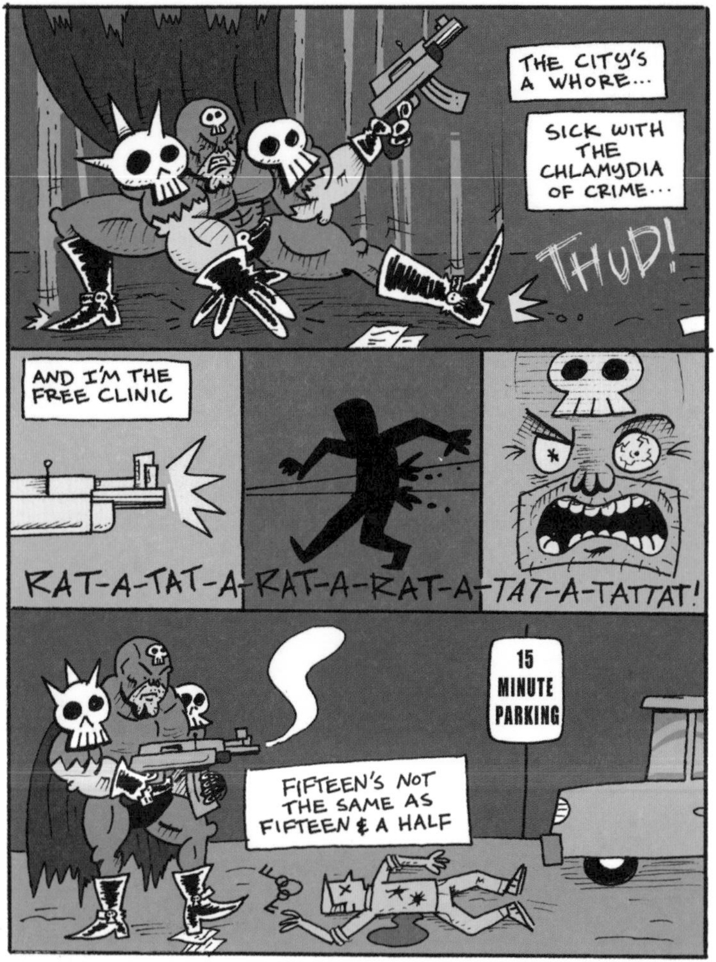
THE CITY'S A WHORE...
SICK WITH THE CHLAMYDIA OF CRIME...
THUD!
AND I'M THE FREE CLINIC
RAT-A-TAT-A-RAT-A-RAT-A-TAT-A-TATTAT!
15 MINUTE PARKING
FIFTEEN'S NOT THE SAME AS FIFTEEN & A HALF

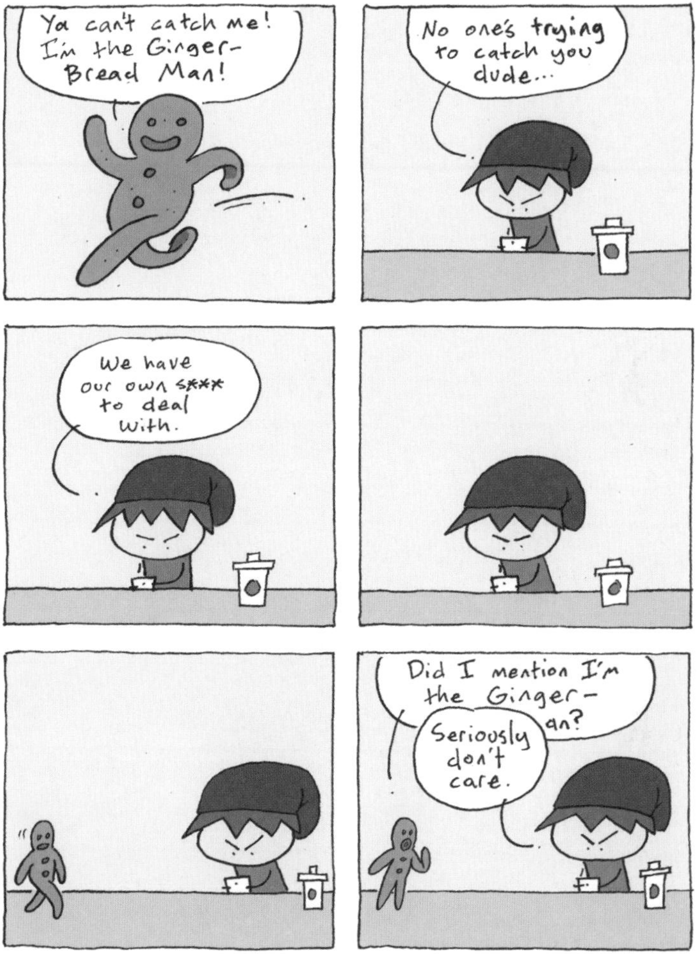
Ya can't catch me! I'm the Ginger-Bread Man!
No one's trying to catch you dude...
We have our own s*** to deal with.
Did I mention I'm the Ginger- an?
Seriously don't care.

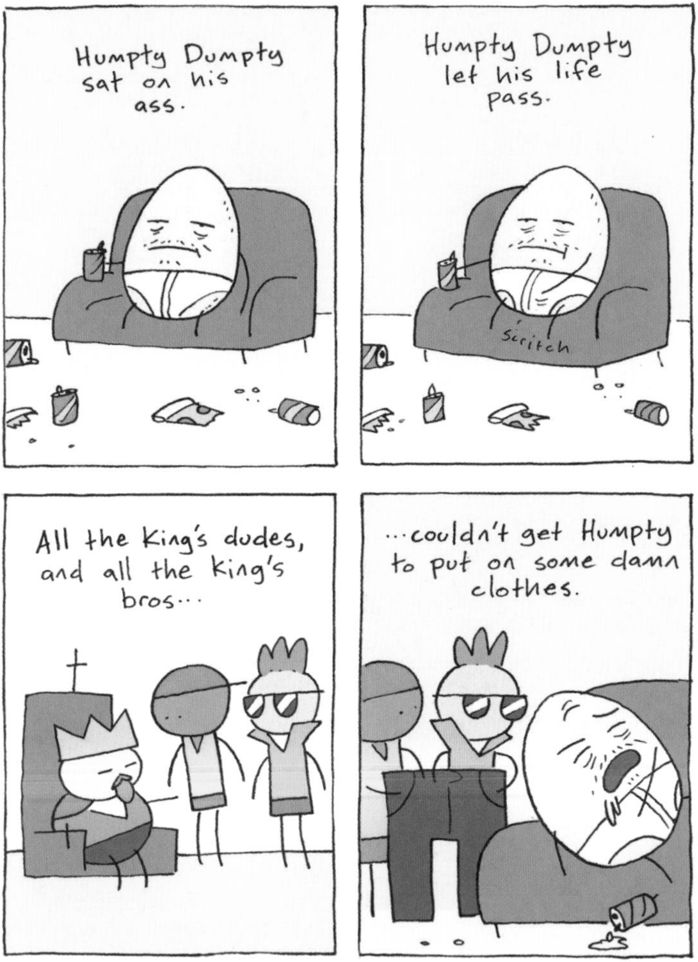
Humpty Dumpty sat on his ass.
Humpty Dumpty let his life pass.
Scritch
All the King's dudes, and all the King's bros...
...couldn't get Humpty to put on some damn clothes.

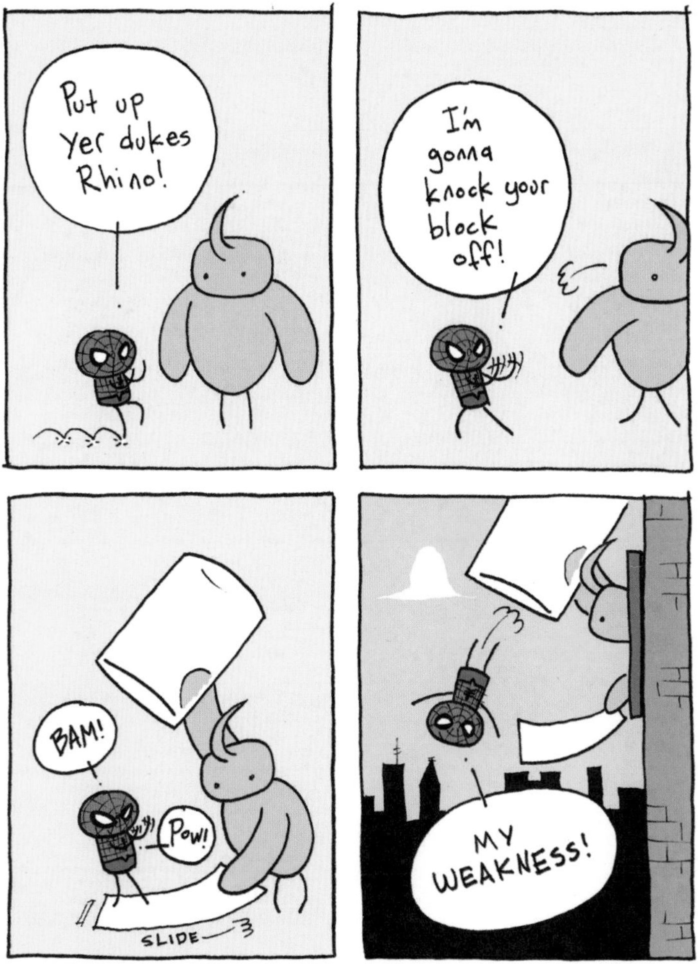
Put up yer dukes Rhino!
I'm gonna knock your block off!
BAM!
POW!
SLIDE
MY WEAKNESS!

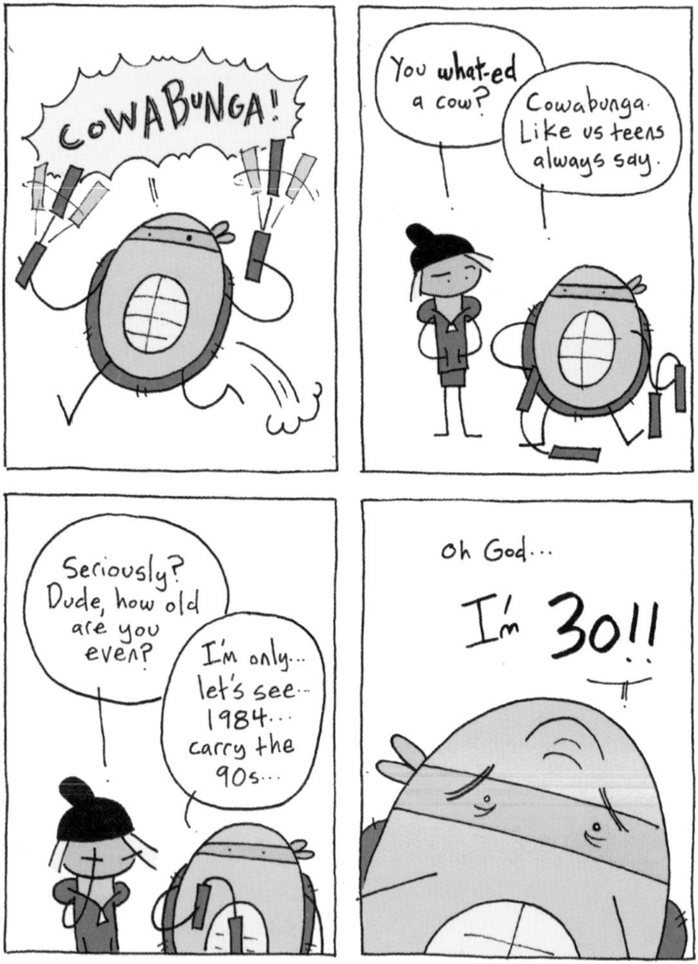
COWABUNGA!
You what-ed a cow?
Cowabunga. Like us teens always say.
Seriously? Dude, how old are you even?
I'm only... let's see... 1984... carry the 90s...
Oh God...
I'm 30!!

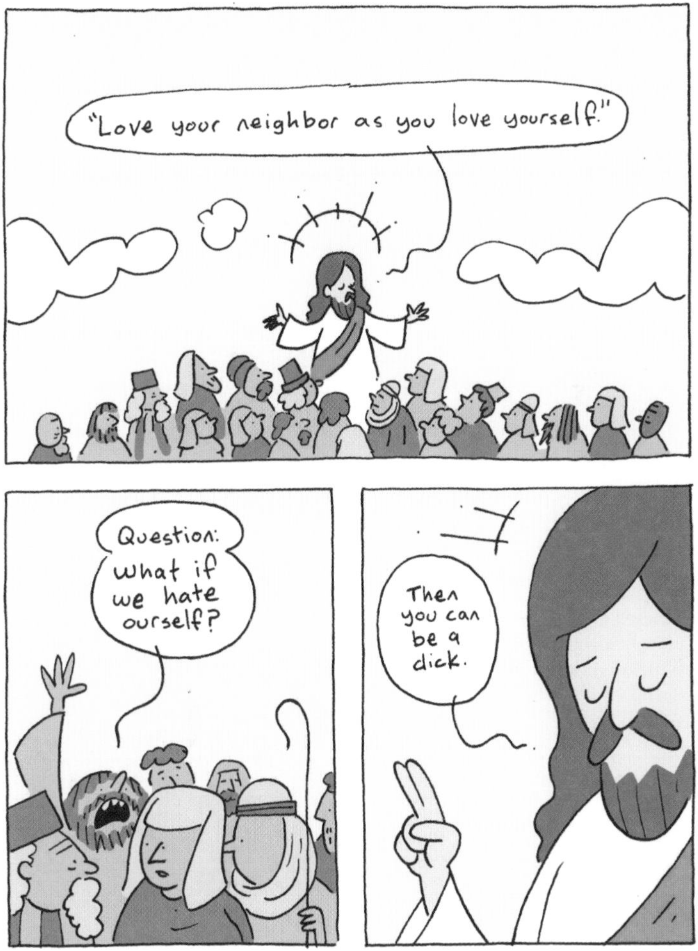
"Love your neighbor as you love yourself."
Question: what if we hate ourself?
Then you can be a dick.

Who met a...

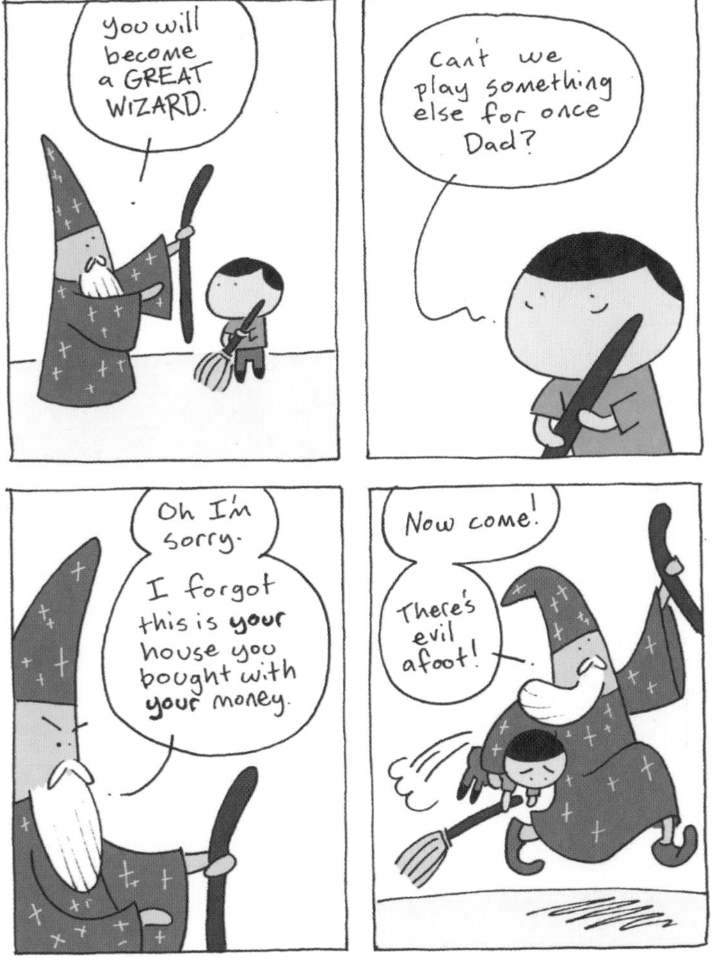
you will become a GREAT WIZARD.
Can't we play something else for once Dad?
Oh I'm sorry.
I forgot this is your house you bought with your money.
Now come!
There's evil afoot!

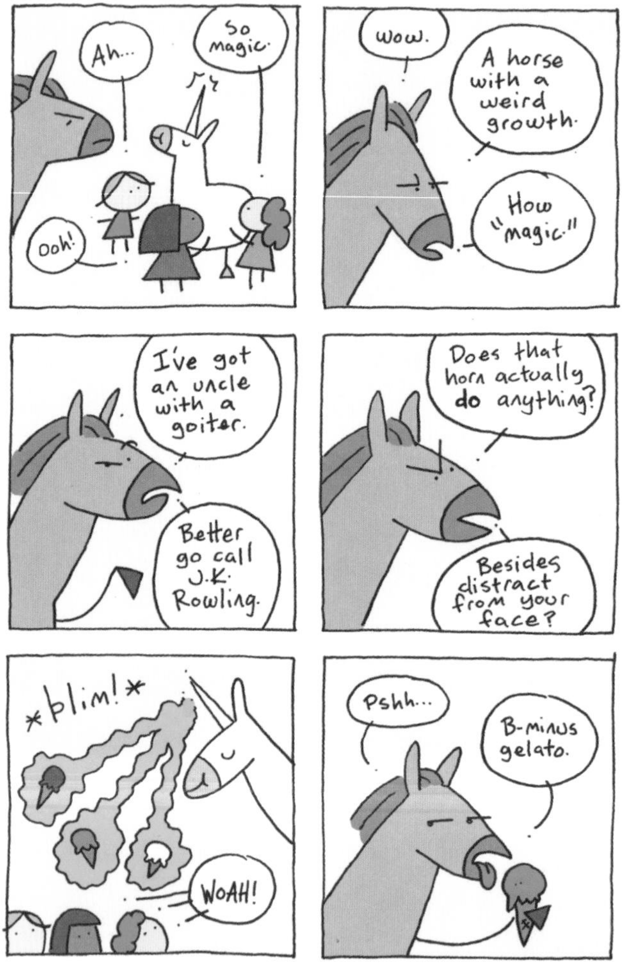
Ah...
So magic.
Ooh!
Wow.
A horse with a weird growth.
How "magic."
I've got an uncle with a goiter.
Better go call J.K. Rowling.
Does that horn actually do anything?
Besides distract from your face?
blim!
WOAH!
Pshh...
B-minus gelato.

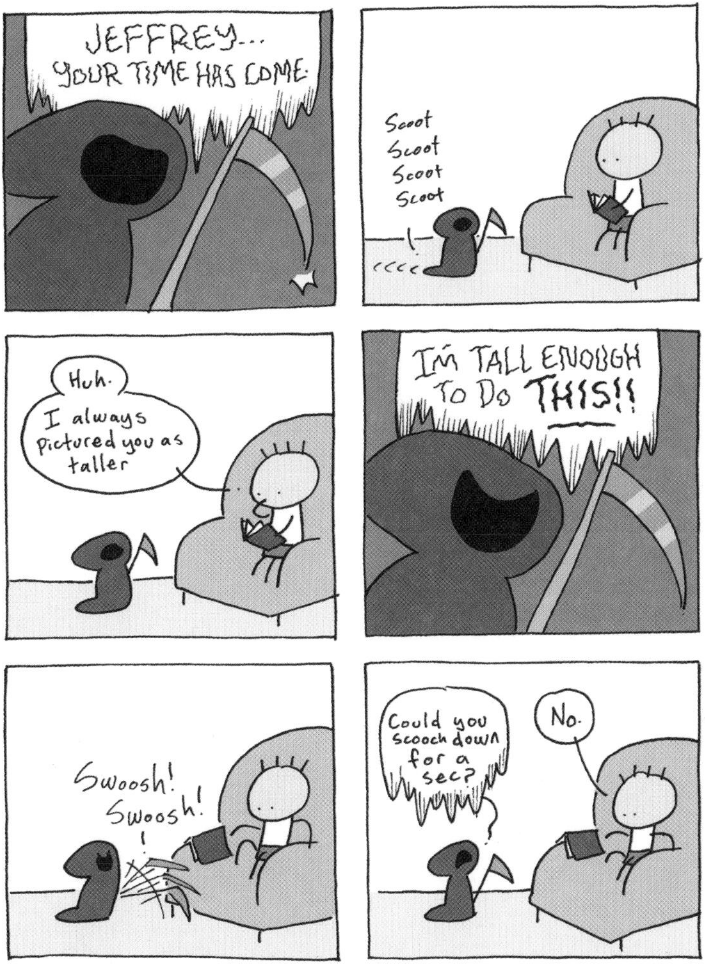
JEFFREY...
YOUR TIME HAS COME.
Scoot
Scoot
Scoot
Scoot
Huh.
I always pictured you as taller
I'M TALL ENOUGH TO DO THIS!!
Swoosh!
Swoosh!
Could you scooch down for a sec?
No.

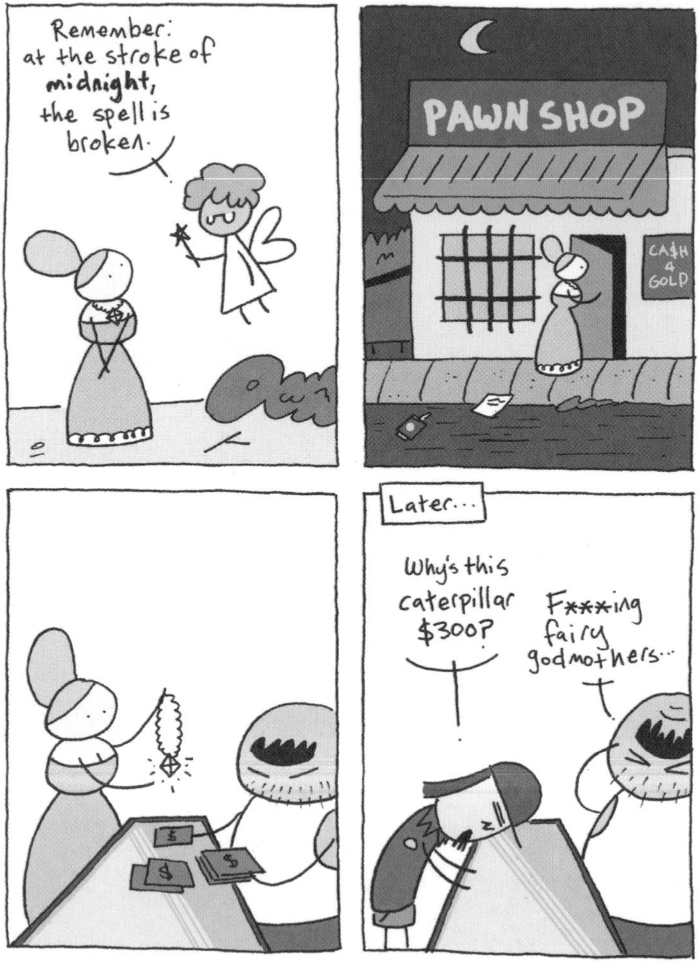
Remember: at the stroke of **midnight**, the spell is broken.
PAWN SHOP
CA$H 4 GOLD
Later...
Why's this caterpillar $300?
F***ing fairy godmothers...

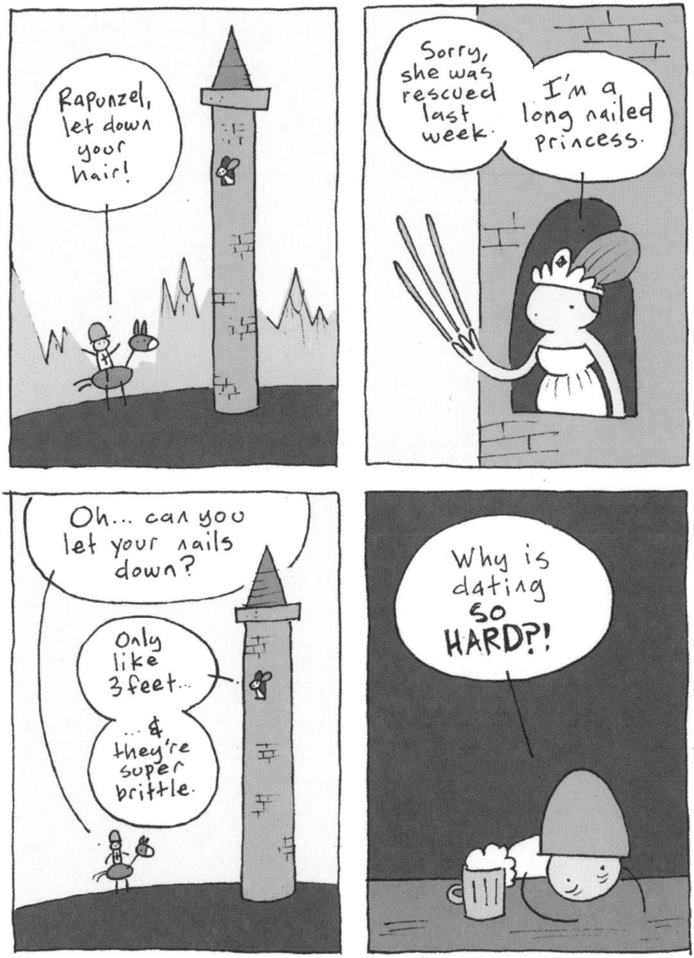
Rapunzel, let down your hair!
Sorry, she was rescued last week.
I'm a long nailed princess.
Oh... can you let your nails down?
Only like 3 feet...
... & they're super brittle.
Why is dating SO HARD?!

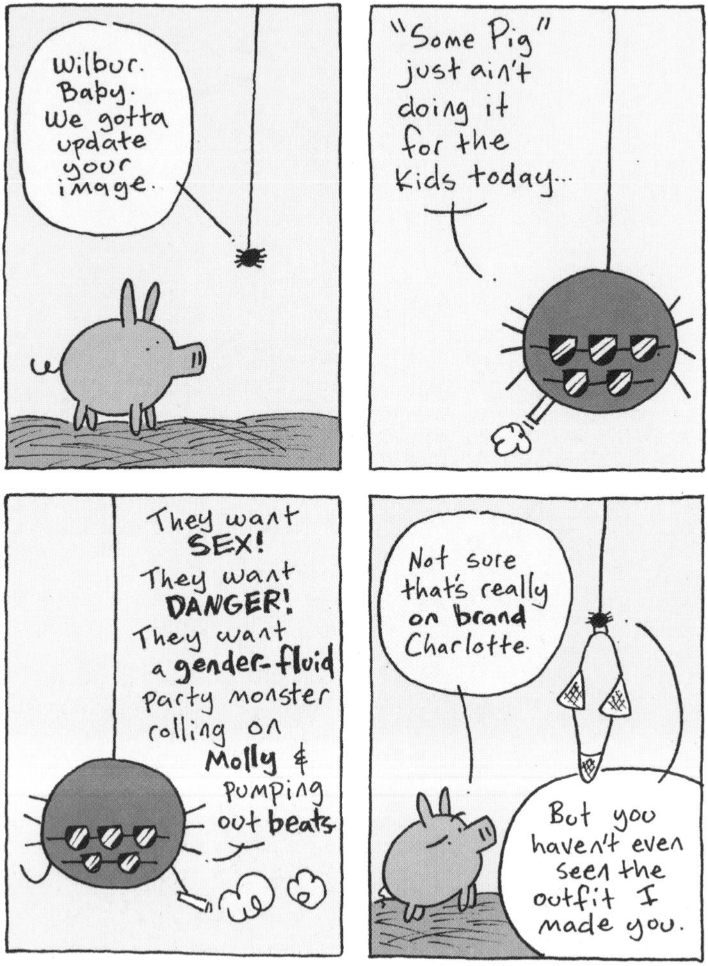
Wilbur. Baby. We gotta update your image.
"Some Pig" just ain't doing it for the kids today...
They want SEX! They want DANGER! They want a gender-fluid party monster rolling on Molly & pumping out beats
Not sure that's really on brand Charlotte.
But you haven't even seen the outfit I made you.

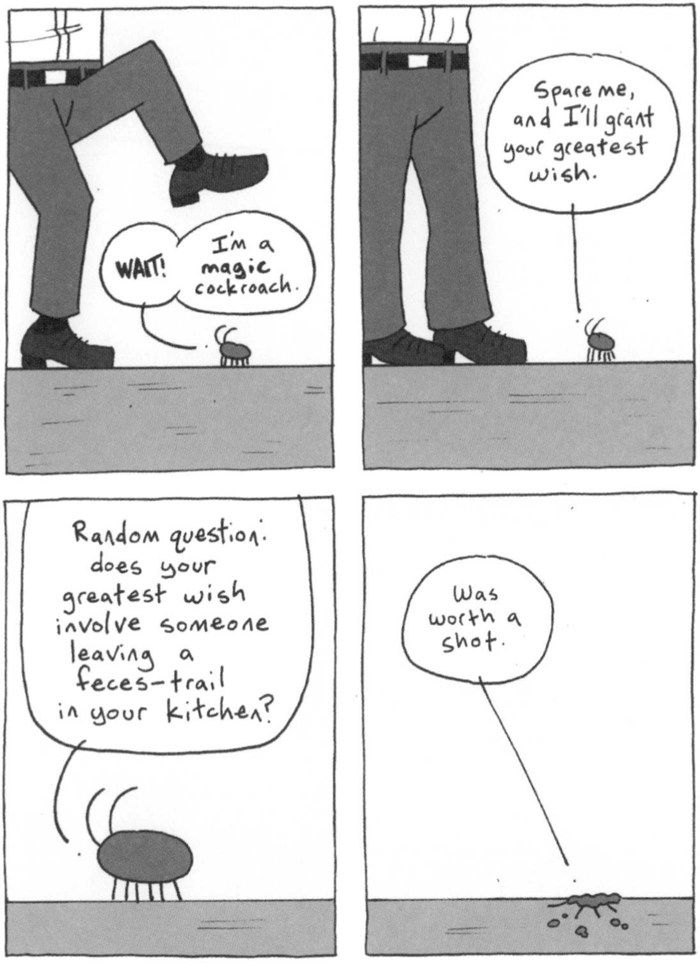
WAIT!
I'm a magic cockroach.
Spare me, and I'll grant your greatest wish.
Random question: does your greatest wish involve someone leaving a feces-trail in your kitchen?
Was worth a shot.

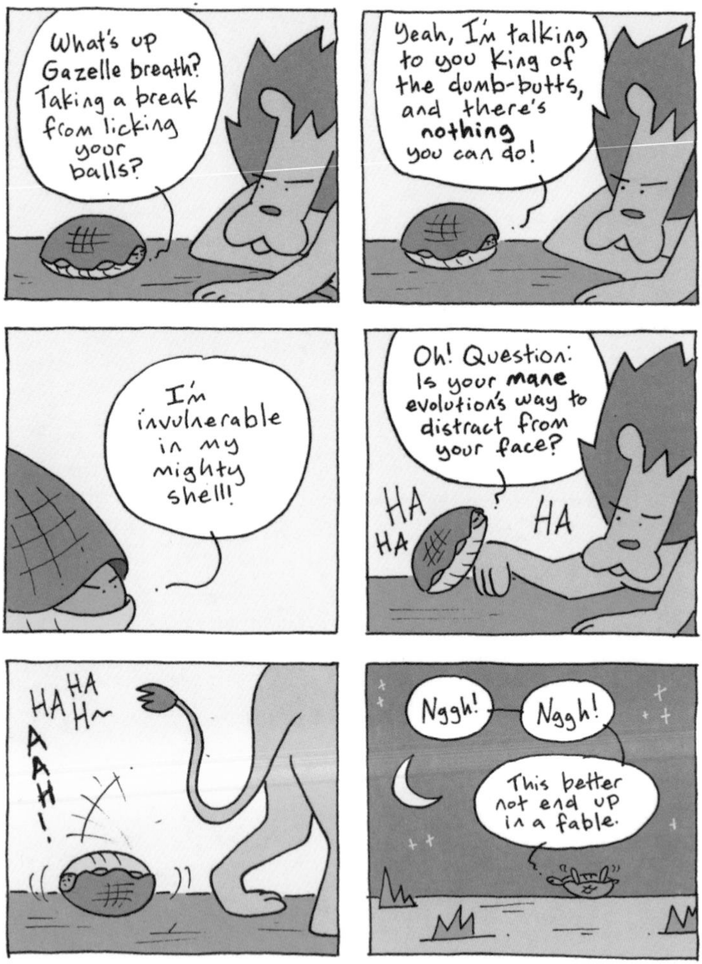
What's up Gazelle breath? Taking a break from licking your balls?
Yeah, I'm talking to you King of the dumb-butts, and there's **nothing** you can do!
I'm invulnerable in my mighty shell!
Oh! Question: Is your **mane** evolution's way to distract from your face?
HA HA
HA
HA HA H~
AAH!
Nggh!
Nggh!
This better not end up in a fable.

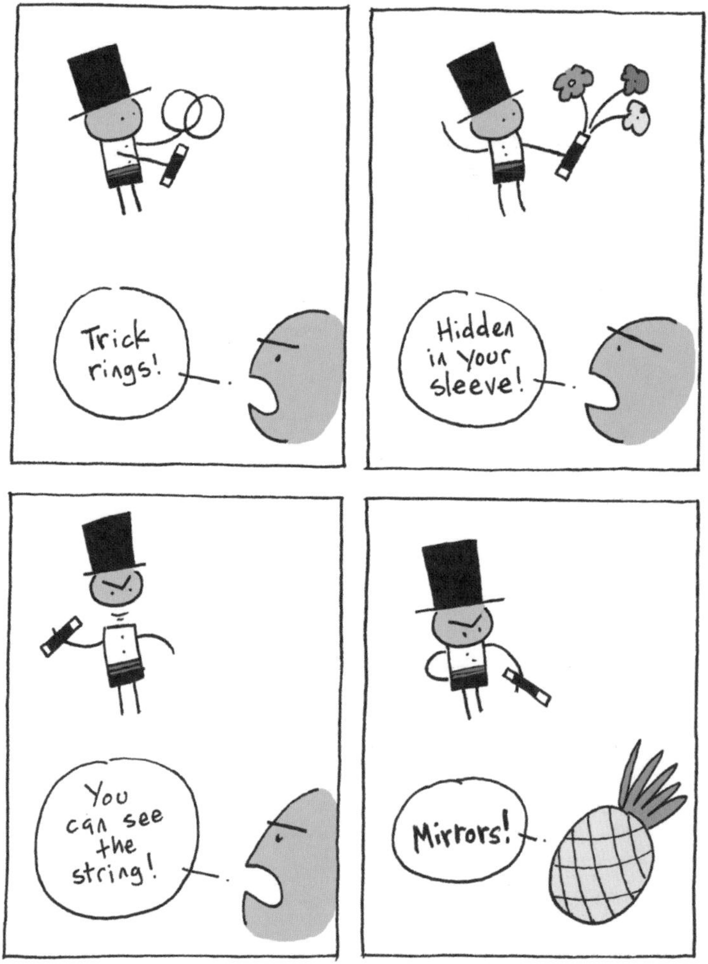
Trick rings!
Hidden in your sleeve!
You can see the string!
Mirrors!

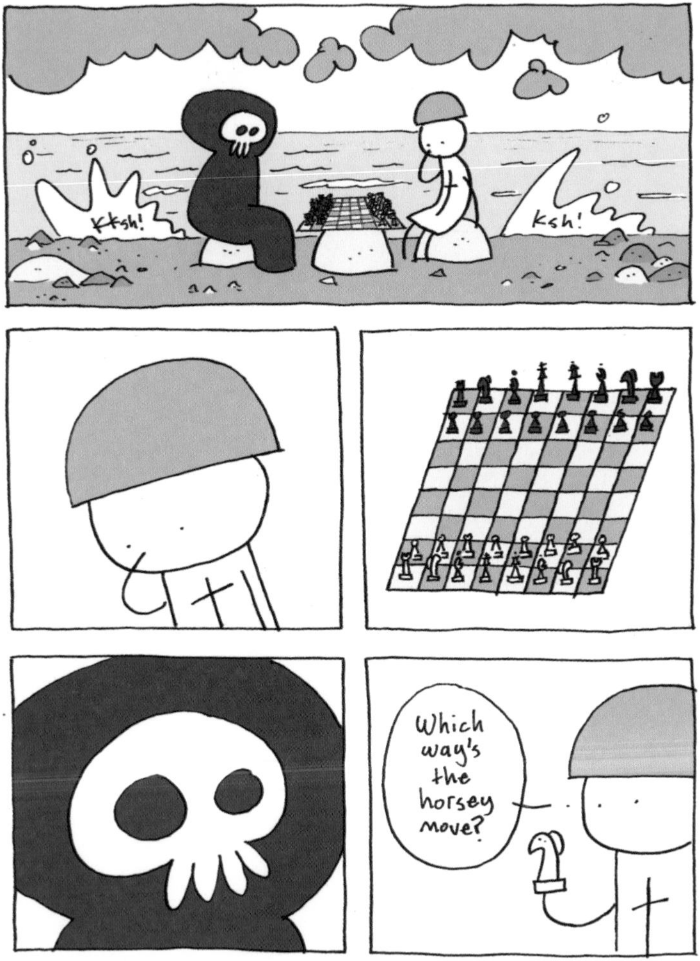
Kksh!
Ksh!
Which way's the horsey move?

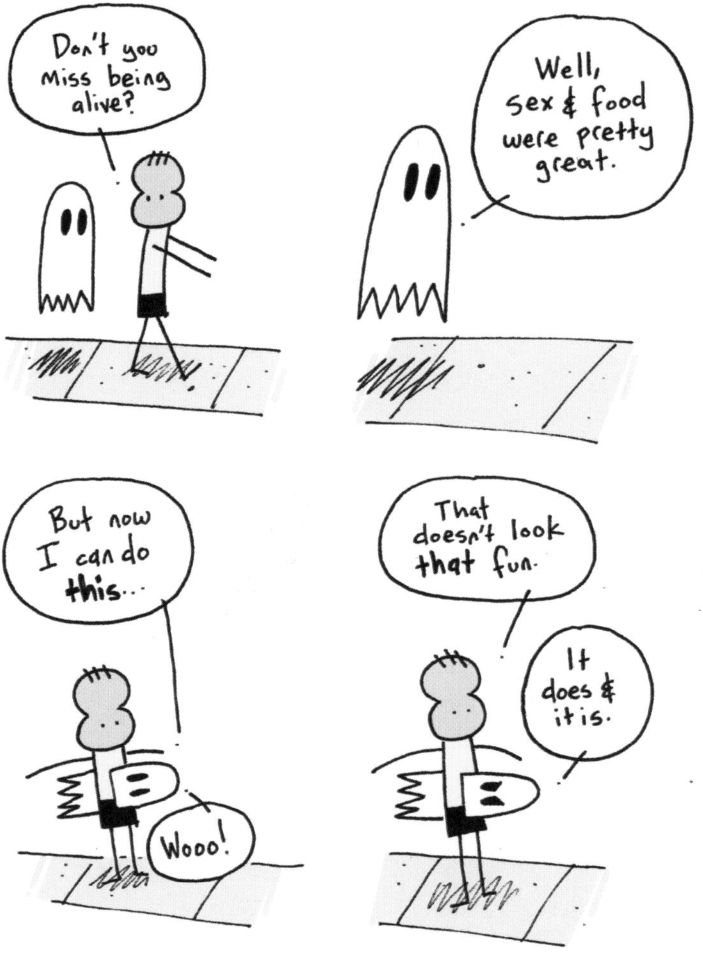

Don't you miss being alive?
Well, sex & food were pretty great.
But now I can do **this**...
Wooo!
That doesn't look **that** fun.
It does & it is.

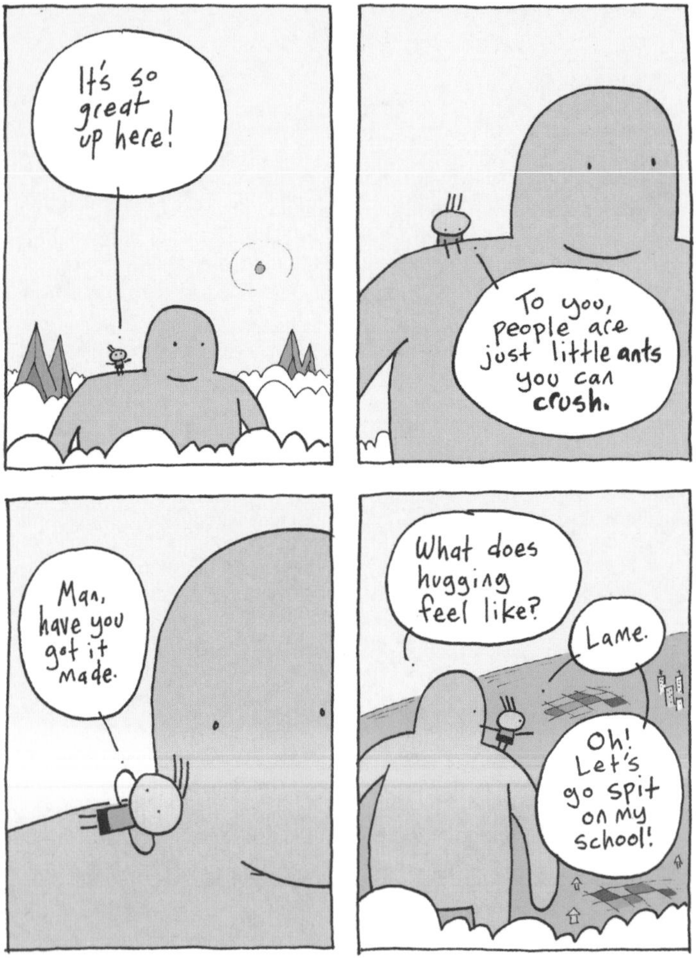
It's so great up here!
To you, people are just little ants you can crush.
Man, have you got it made.
What does hugging feel like?
Lame.
Oh! Let's go spit on my school!

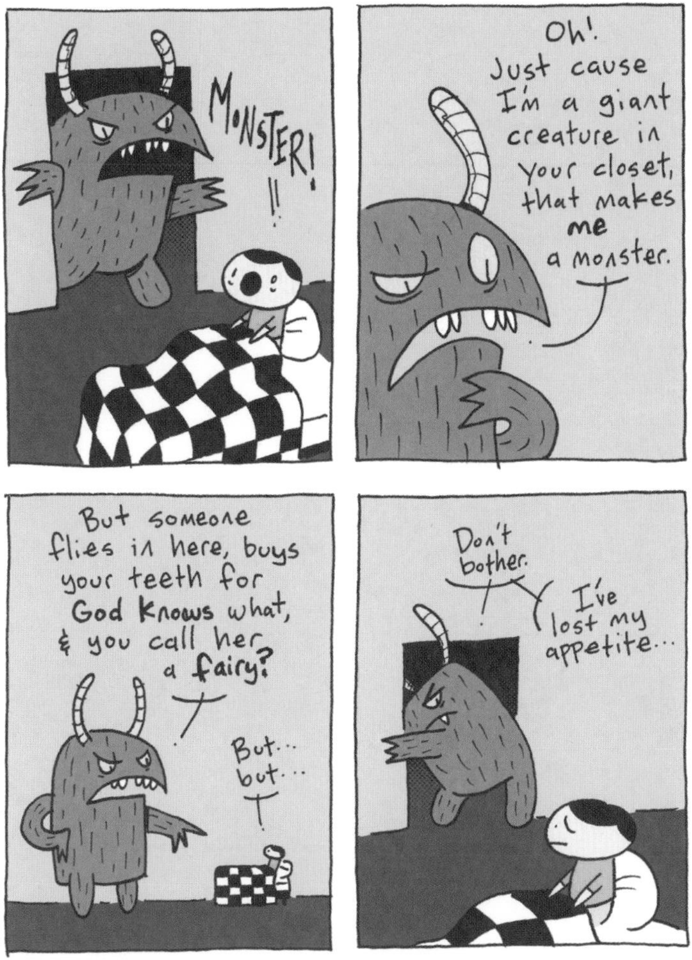
MONSTER!
!!
Oh!
Just cause I'm a giant creature in your closet, that makes **me** a monster.
But someone flies in here, buys your teeth for **God knows** what, & you call her a **fairy?**
But... but...
Don't bother.
I've lost my appetite...

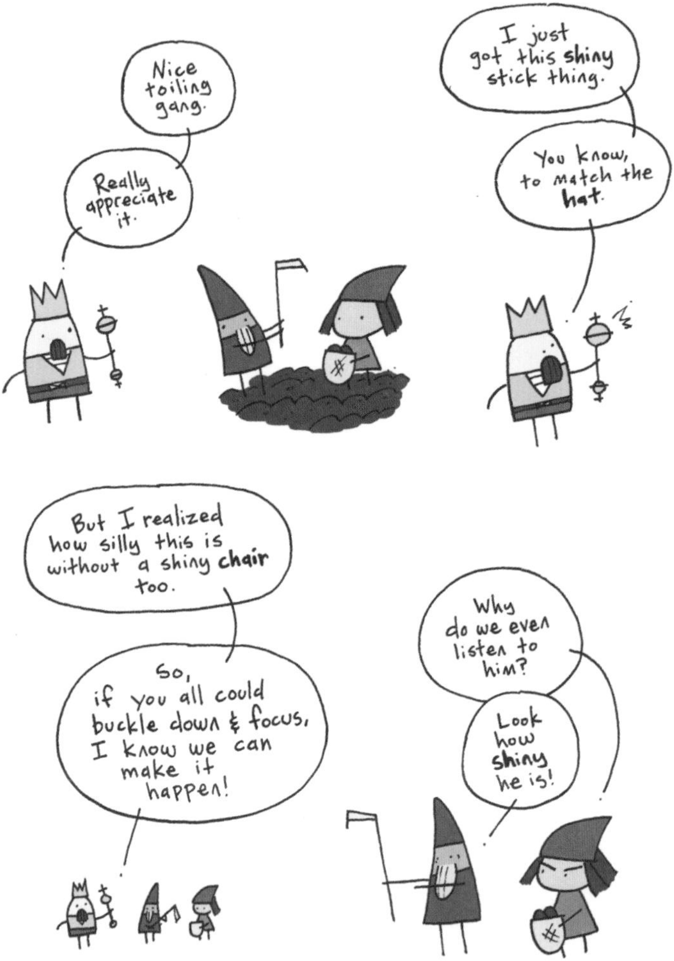
Nice toiling gang.
Really appreciate it.
I just got this shiny stick thing.
You know, to match the hat.
But I realized how silly this is without a shiny chair too.
So, if you all could buckle down & focus, I know we can make it happen!
Why do we even listen to him?
Look how shiny he is!

Remember Corey, be careful what you wish for...
Care's for Pussies. Make my hands LASERS!
Poof!
Woo!
LASERS!
LATER...
Well Corey, I hope destroying the world taught you a...
LASERS!

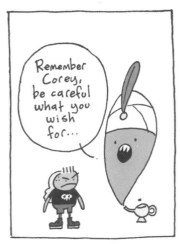

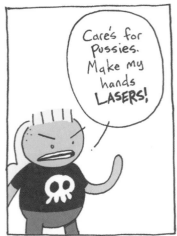

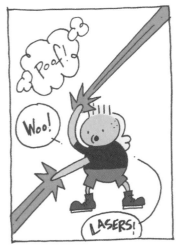

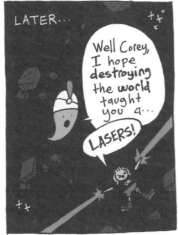

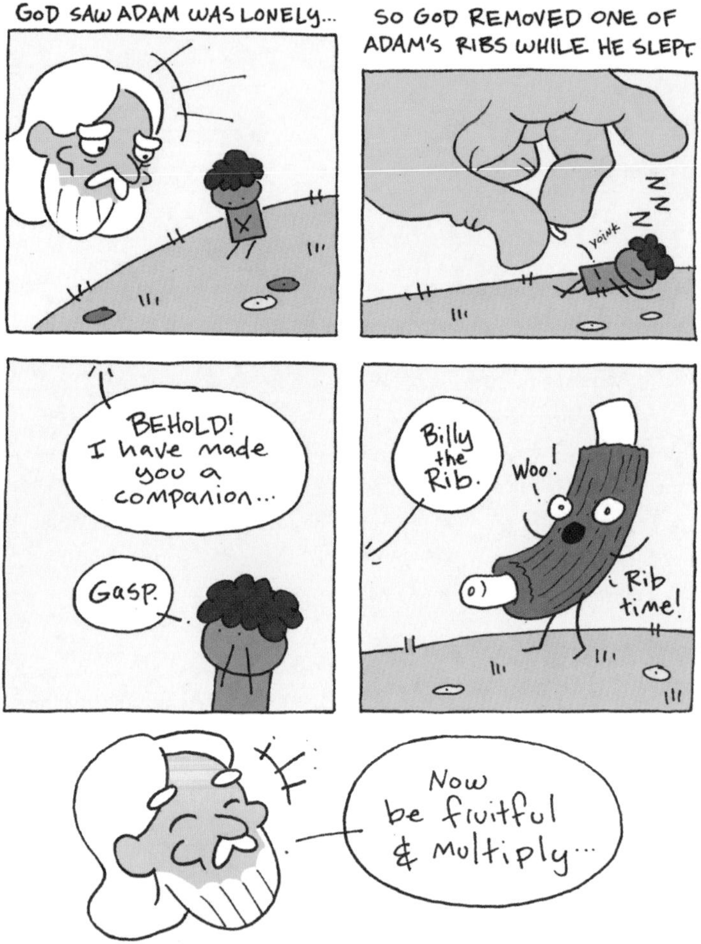
GOD SAW ADAM WAS LONELY...
SO GOD REMOVED ONE OF ADAM'S RIBS WHILE HE SLEPT.
YOINK
Z Z Z
BEHOLD! I have made you a companion...
Gasp.
Billy the Rib.
Woo!
¡Rib time!
Now be fruitful & multiply...

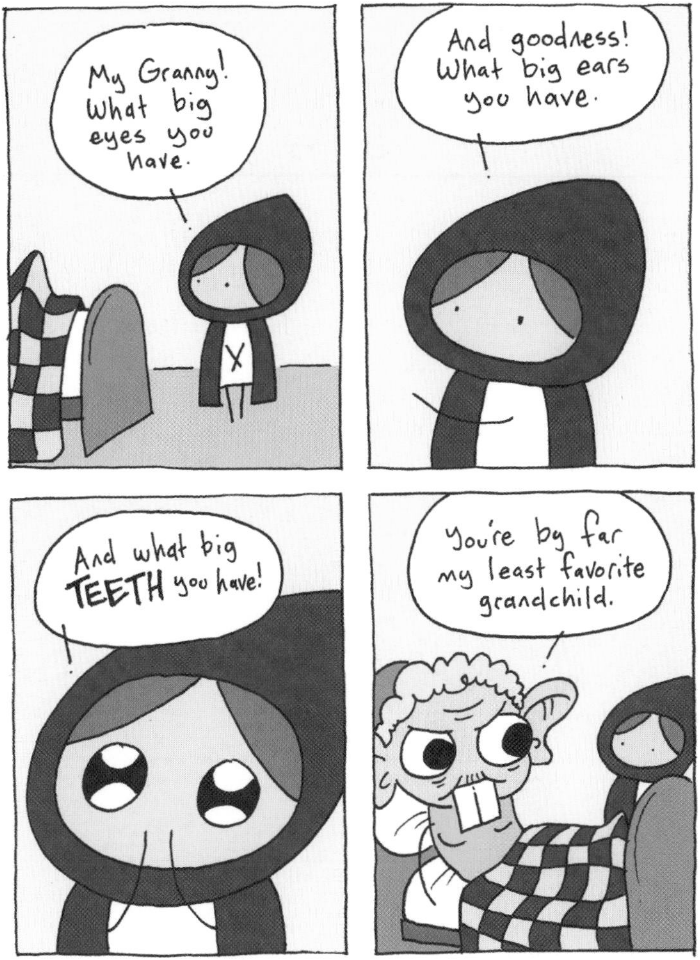
My Granny! What big eyes you have.
And goodness! What big ears you have.
And what big TEETH you have!
You're by far my least favorite grandchild.

Until one day...

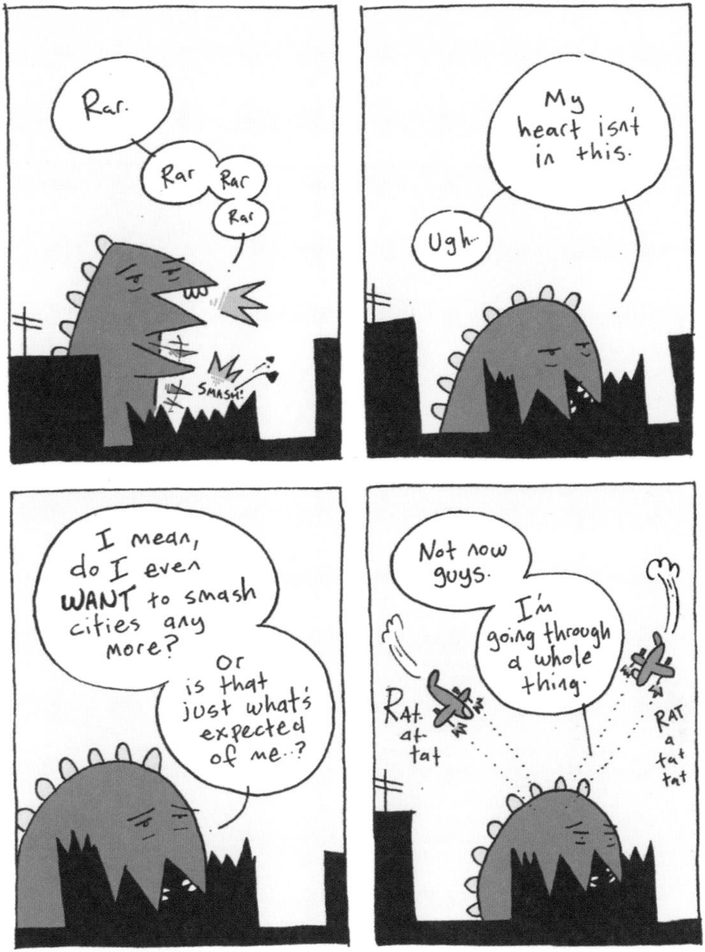
Rar.
Rar
Rar
Rar
SMASH!
My heart isn't in this.
Ugh...
I mean, do I even WANT to smash cities any more?
Or is that just what's expected of me..?
Not now guys.
I'm going through a whole thing.
RAT-at-tat
RAT a tat tat

CHOOSE YOUR OWN ADVENTURE

① You approach the dragon's cave.

Enter the cave (Panel 7)
Figure out if this is what you want
to do with your life (Panel 2)

② You never really wanted to slay dragons. Your father pushed you into it.

Enter the cave (Panel 7)
Confront your father (Panel 3)

③ "I wasn't built for slaying poppa. I was built for pottery!"

He's unenthusiastic.

Enter the cave (Panel 7)
Screw him! Follow your dream
(Panel 4)

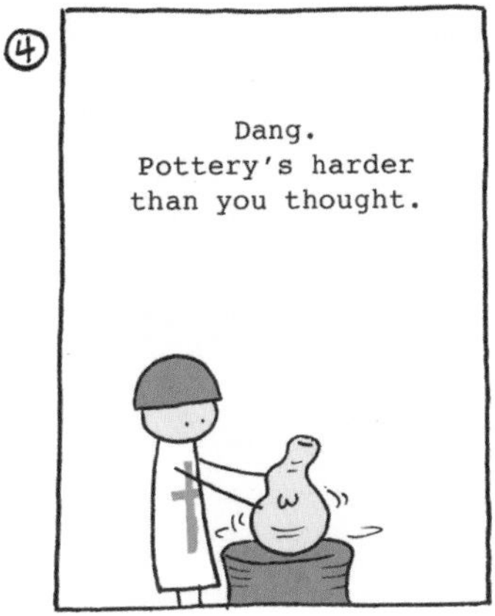
Dang.
Pottery's harder
than you thought.

Enter the cave (Panel 7)
Keep trying (Panel 5)

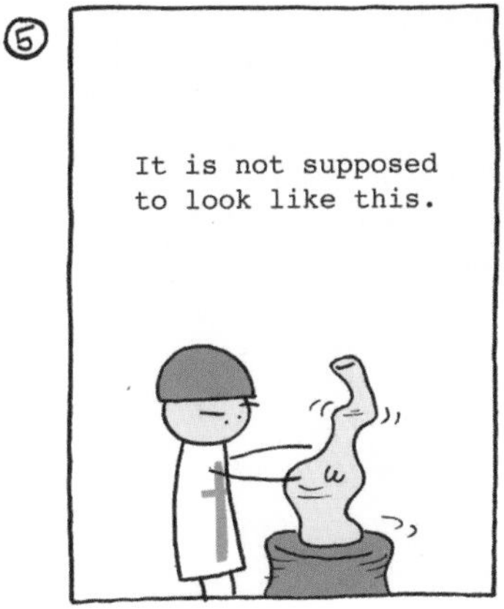
It is not supposed
to look like this.

Enter the cave (Panel 7)
Maybe spin the wheel faster (Panel 6)

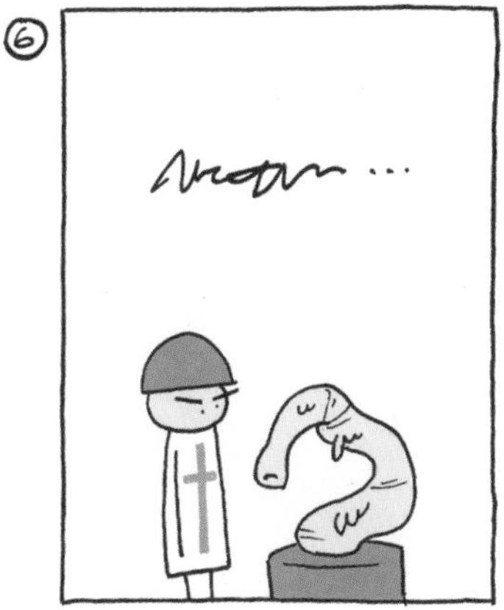

F**K it. Enter the cave
(Panel 7)

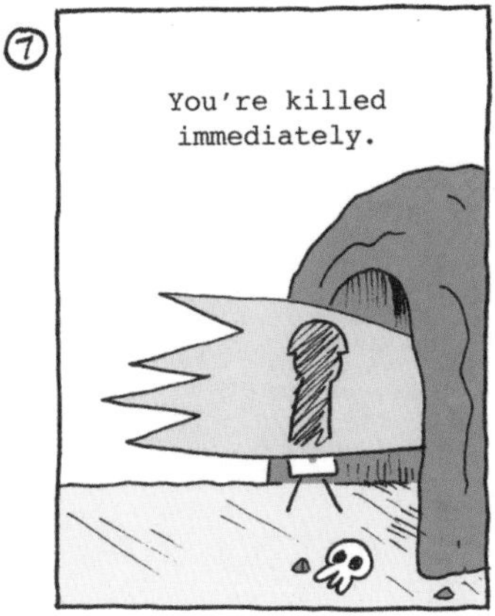
You're killed
immediately.

Hey, are you one of those kids who can see ghosts?
Uh... I guess so.
Found one!
over here.
Hey
hey
Look at me
Hey
hey
(Hey.
(Hey
The dead sure are needy.
Lookit
Hey

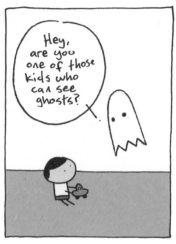

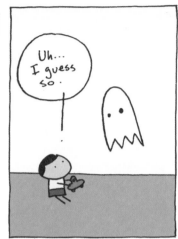

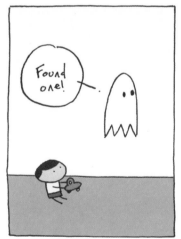

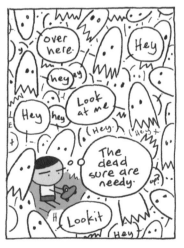

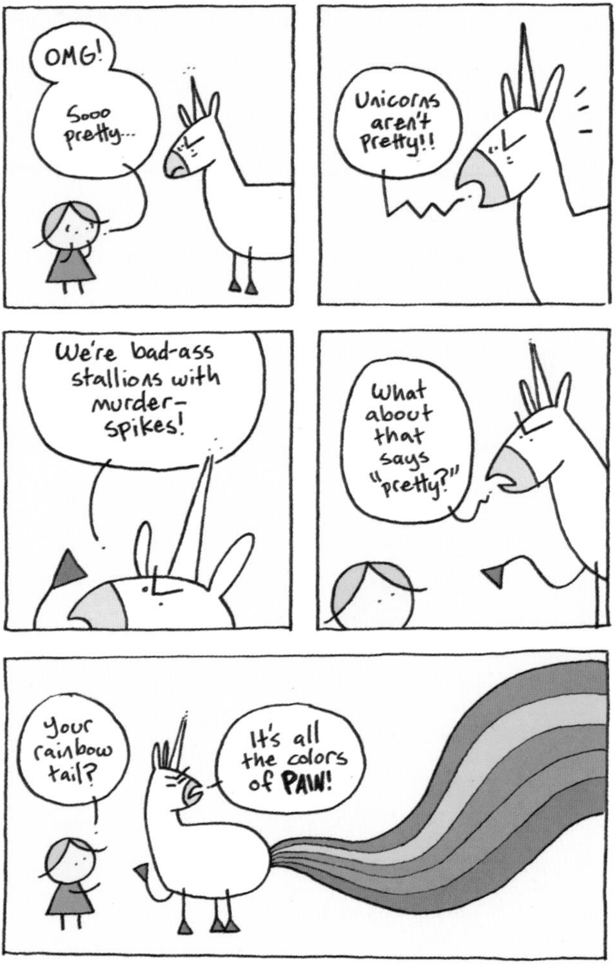
OMG!
Sooo pretty...
Unicorns aren't Pretty!!
We're bad-ass stallions with murder-spikes!
What about that says "pretty?"
Your rainbow tail?
It's all the colors of PAIN!

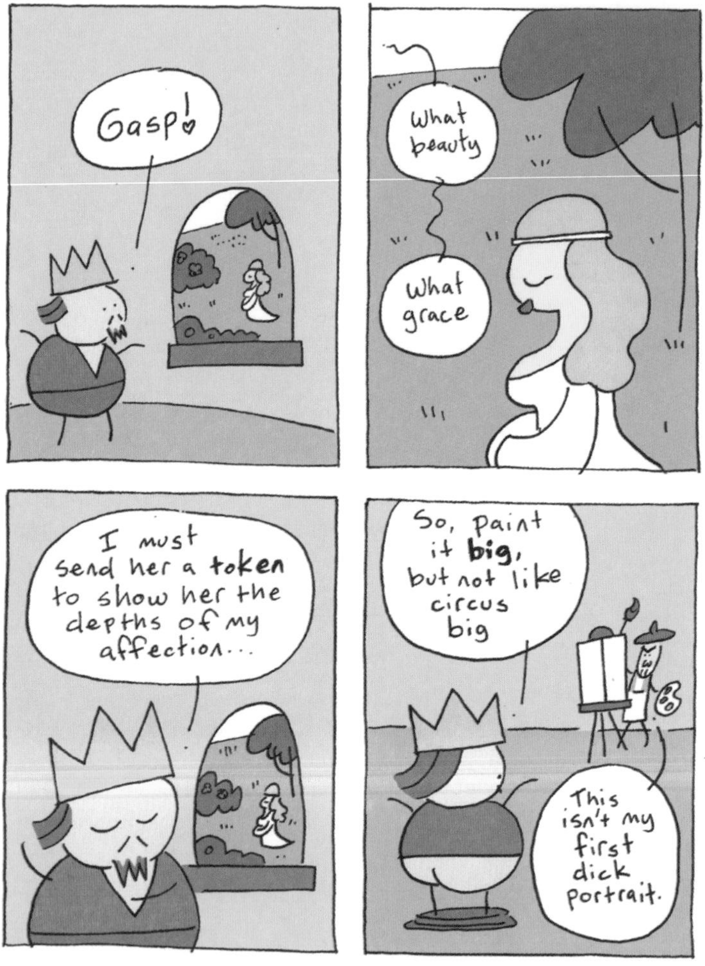
Gasp!
What beauty
What grace
I must send her a **token** to show her the depths of my affection...
So, paint it **big**, but not like circus big
This isn't my first dick portrait.

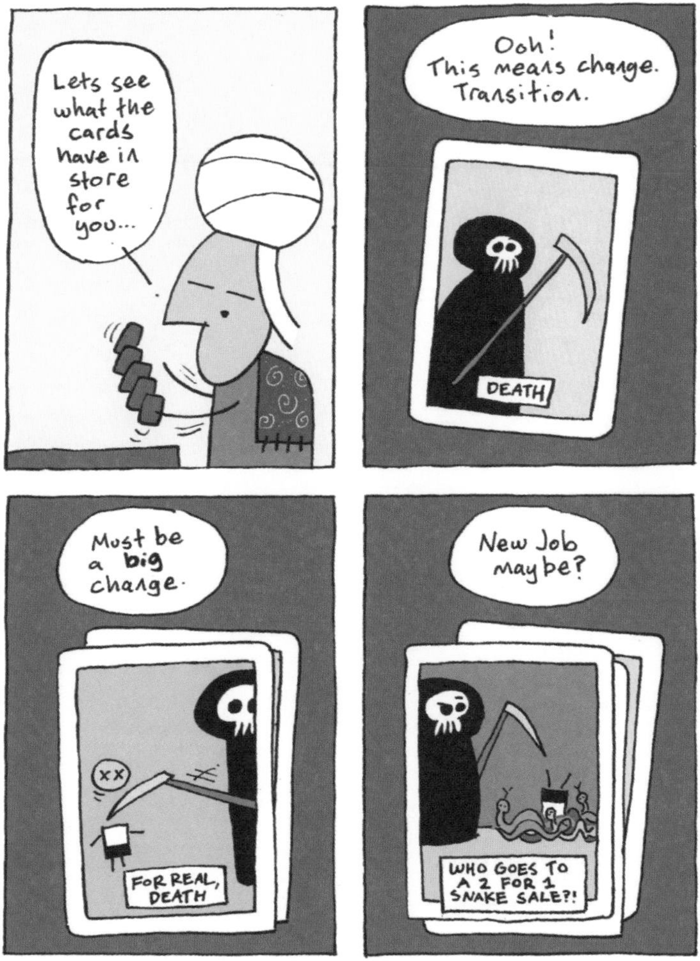
Lets see what the cards have in store for you...
Ooh! This means change. Transition.
DEATH
Must be a **big** change.
FOR REAL, DEATH
New Job maybe?
WHO GOES TO A 2 FOR 1 SNAKE SALE?!

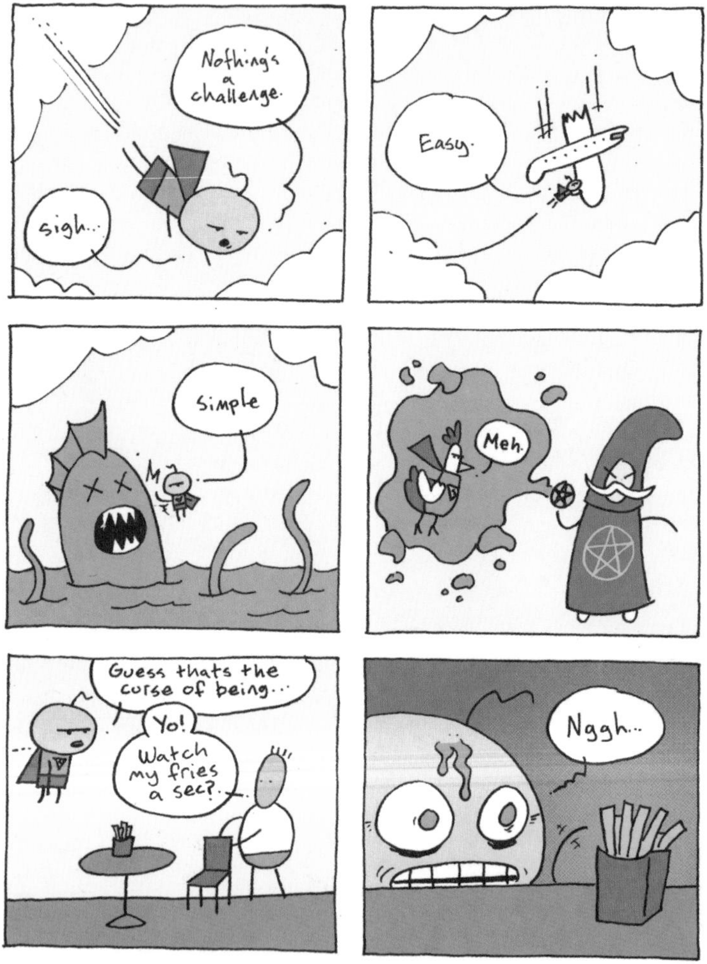
Nothing's a challenge.
sigh...
Easy.
Simple
Meh.
Guess thats the curse of being...
Yo! Watch my fries a sec?
Nggh...

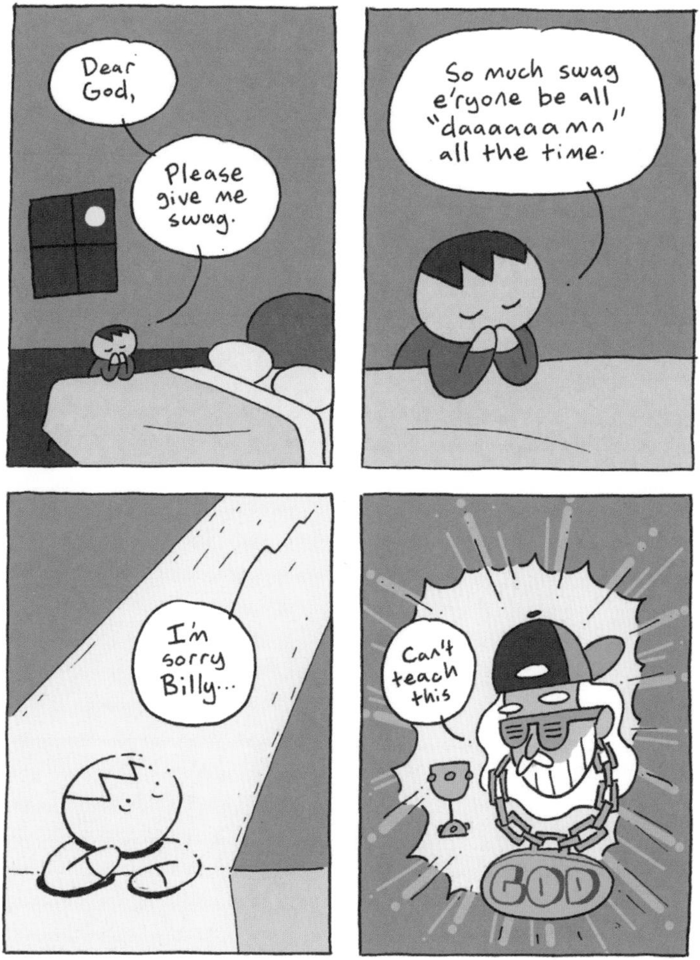

Dear God,
Please give me swag.
So much swag e'ryone be all "daaaaaamn" all the time.
I'm sorry Billy...
Can't teach this
GOD

WoLF!
WoLF!
Wait...
There's no wolf here.
That's clearly a coyote.
h Grrrr
No one likes a liar son.
Scrrrrt...

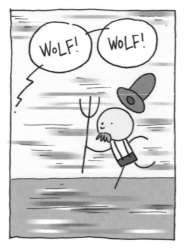

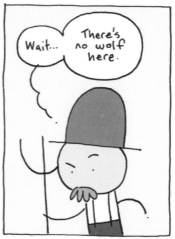

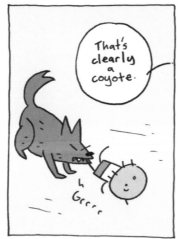

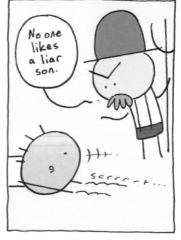

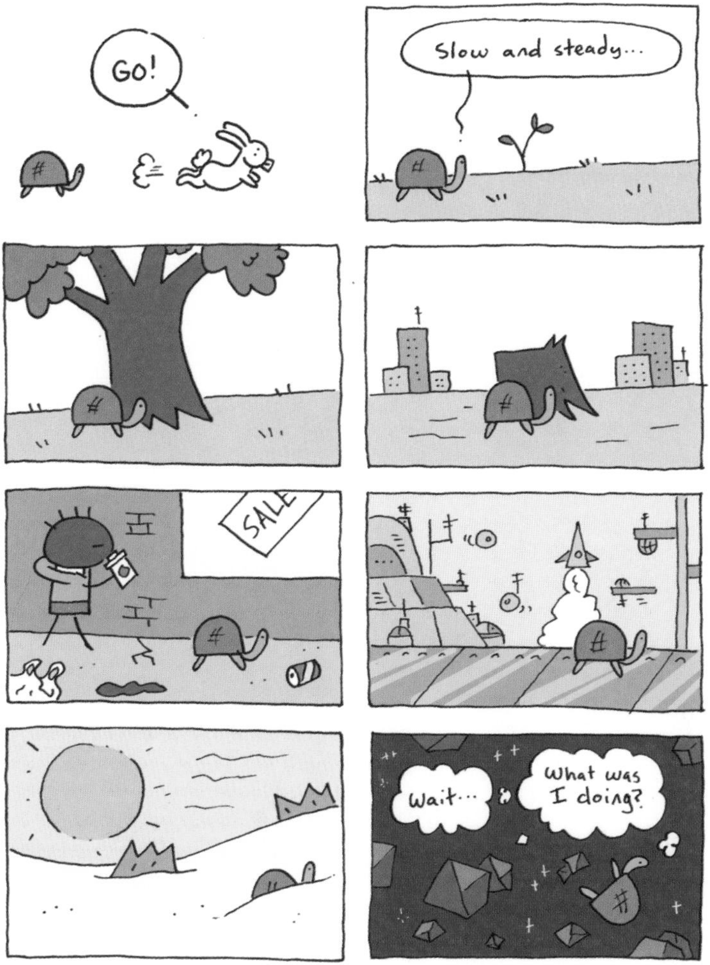
GO!
Slow and steady...
SALE
Wait...
What was I doing?

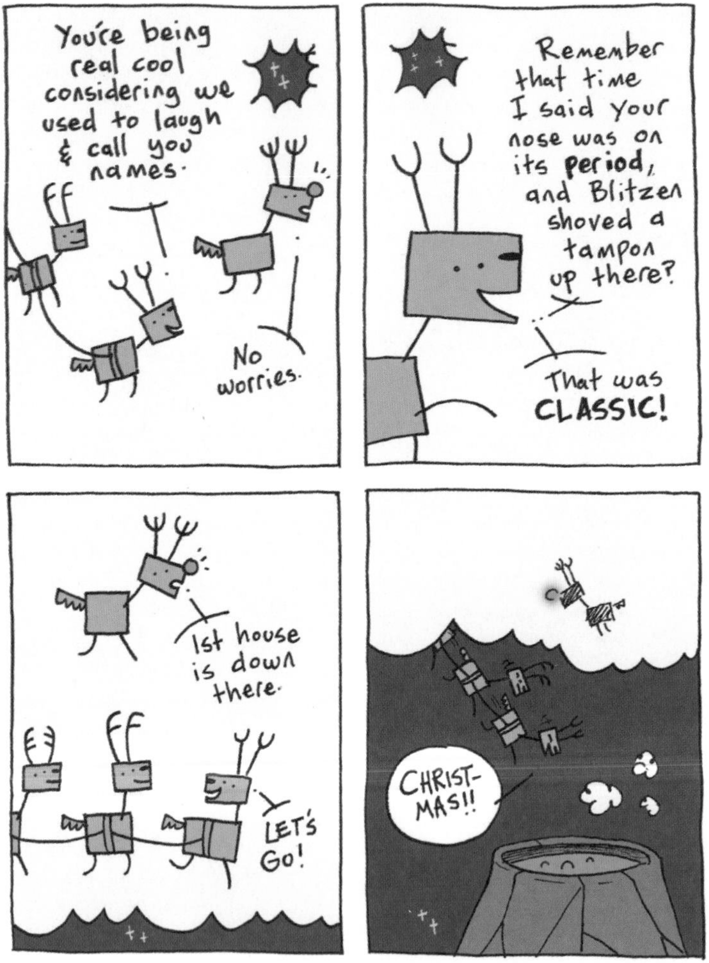
You're being real cool considering we used to laugh & call you names.
No worries.
Remember that time I said your nose was on its **period**, and Blitzen shoved a tampon up there?
That was **CLASSIC!**
1st house is down there.
LET'S GO!
CHRIST-MAS!!

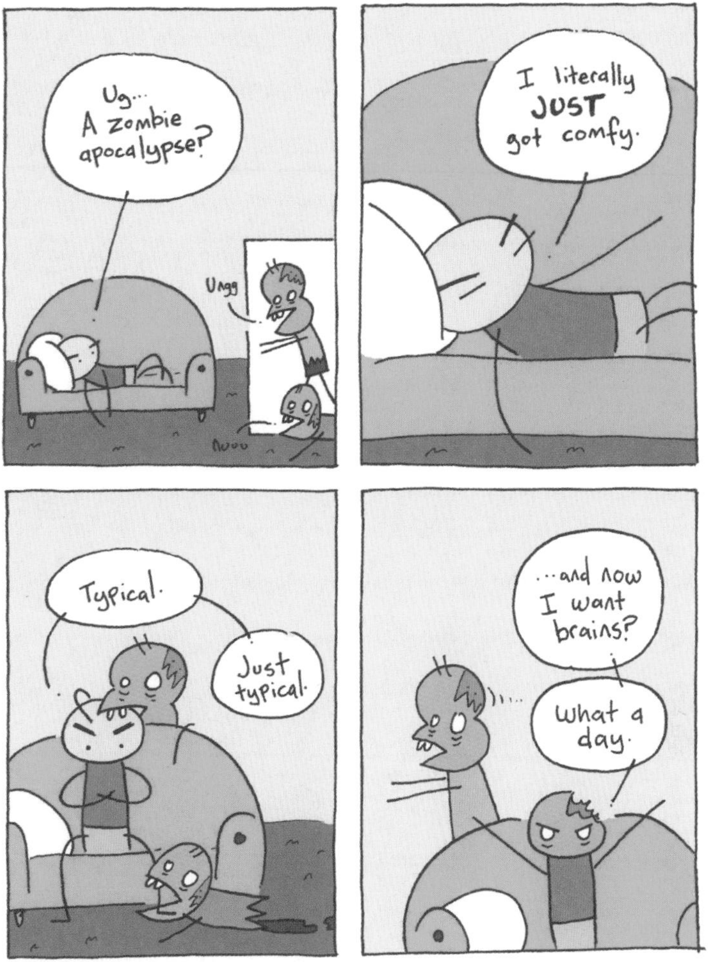
Ug...
A zombie
apocalypse?
Ungg
Nooo
I literally
JUST
got comfy.
Typical.
Just
typical.
...and now
I want
brains?
What a
day.

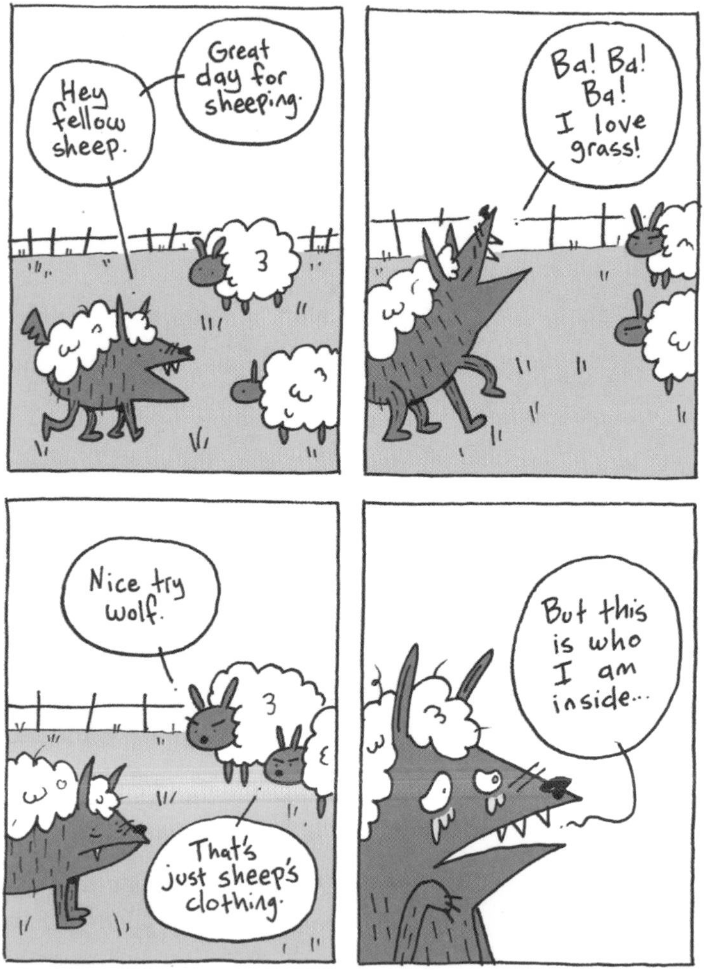
Hey fellow sheep.
Great day for sheeping.
Ba! Ba! Ba! I love grass!
Nice try wolf.
That's just sheep's clothing.
But this is who I am inside...

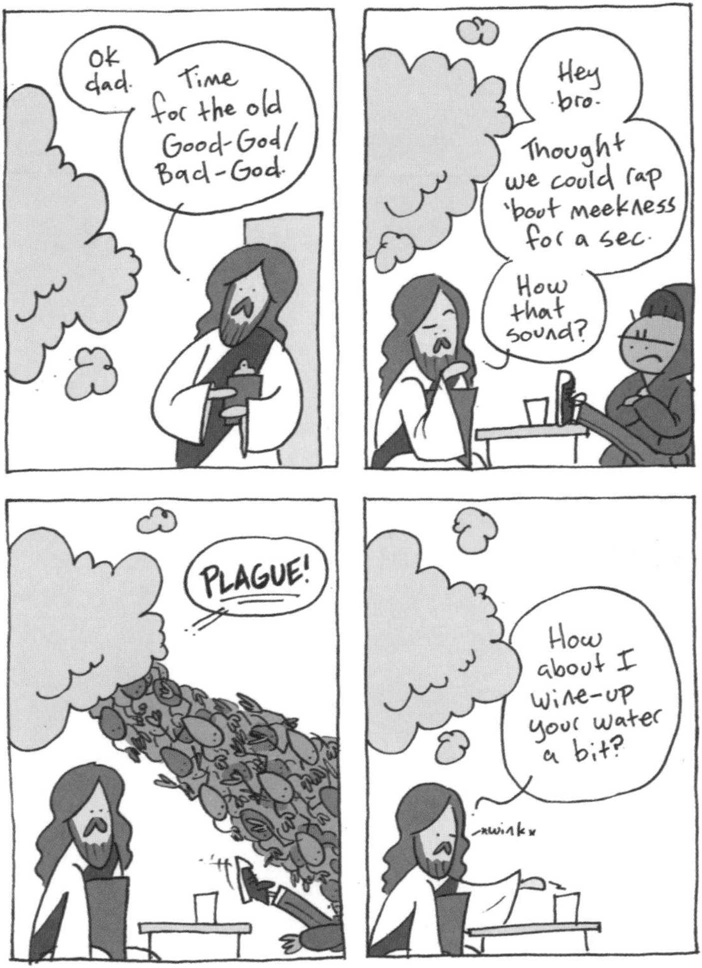
Ok dad.
Time for the old Good-God/Bad-God.
Hey bro.
Thought we could rap 'bout meekness for a sec.
How that sound?
PLAGUE!
How about I wine-up your water a bit?
wink

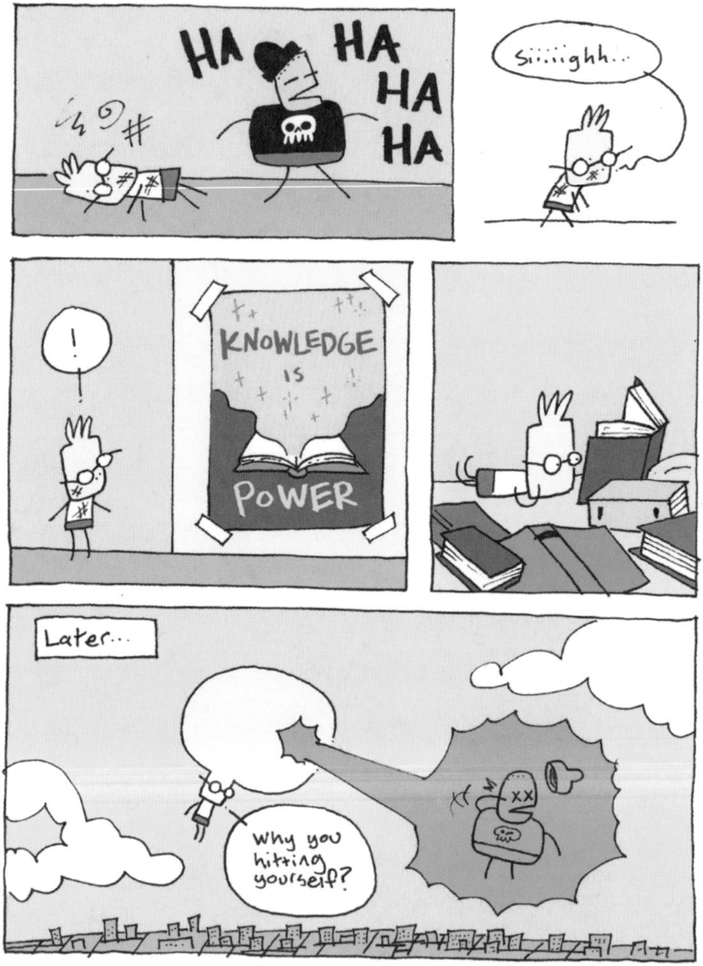
HA HA HA HA
Siiiighh...
!
KNOWLEDGE IS POWER
Later...
Why you hitting yourself?

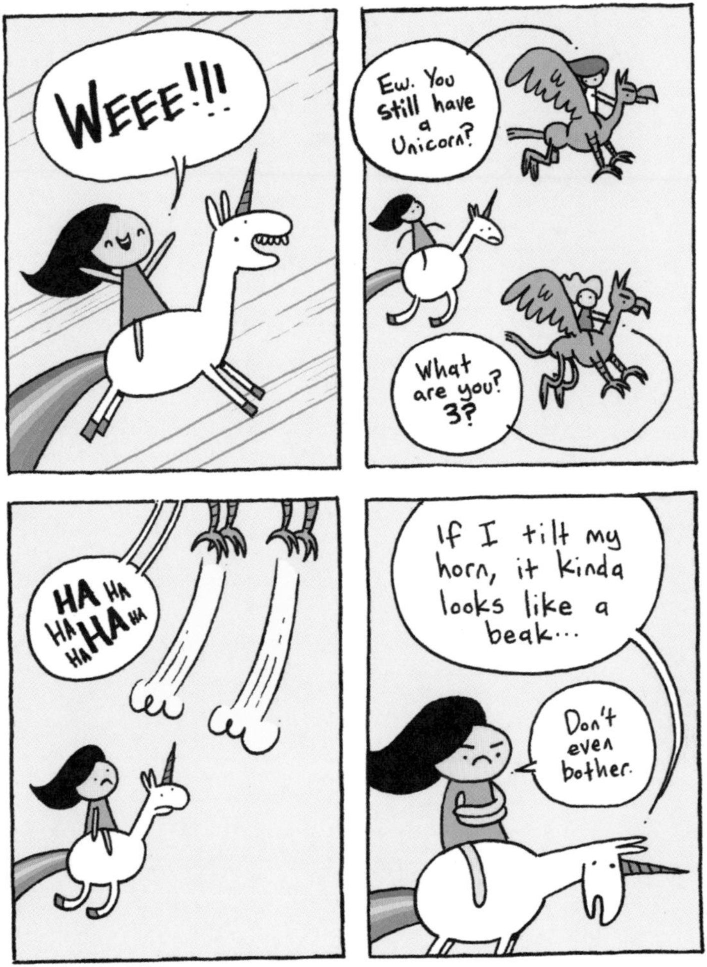
WEEE!!!
Ew. You still have a Unicorn?
What are you? 3?
HA HA HA HA HA HA
If I tilt my horn, it kinda looks like a beak...
Don't even bother.

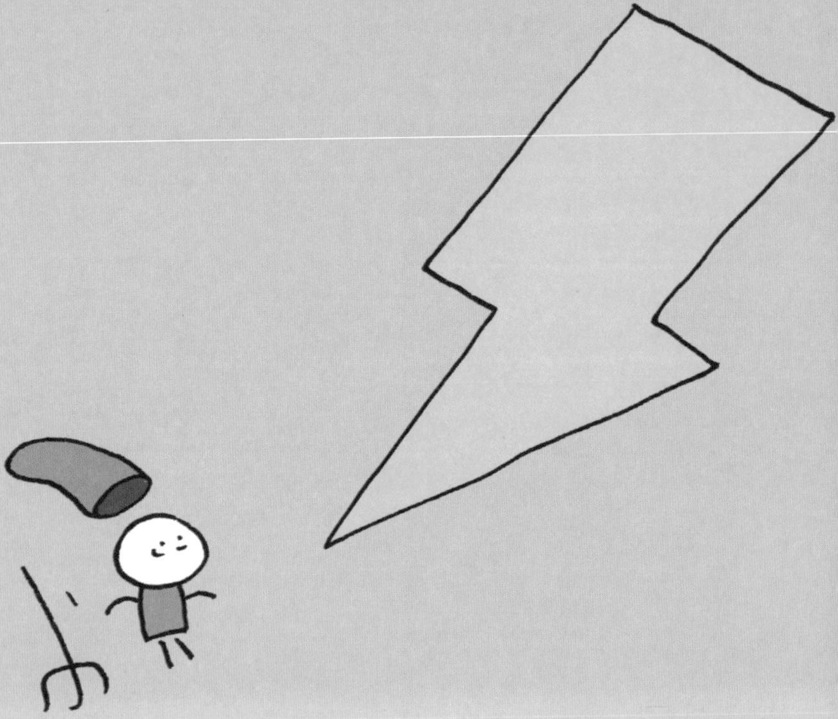

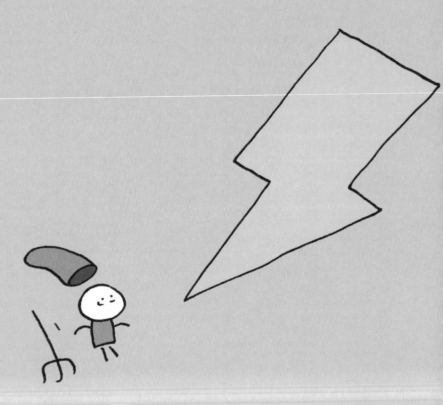

But suddenly...

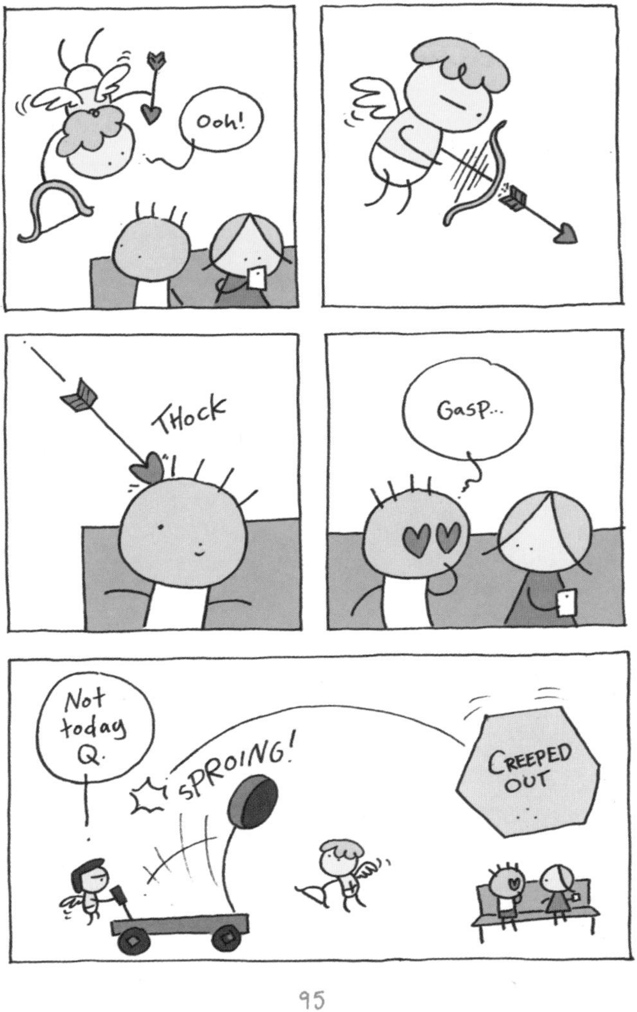
Ooh!
THOCK
Gasp...
Not today Q.
SPROING!
CREEPED OUT

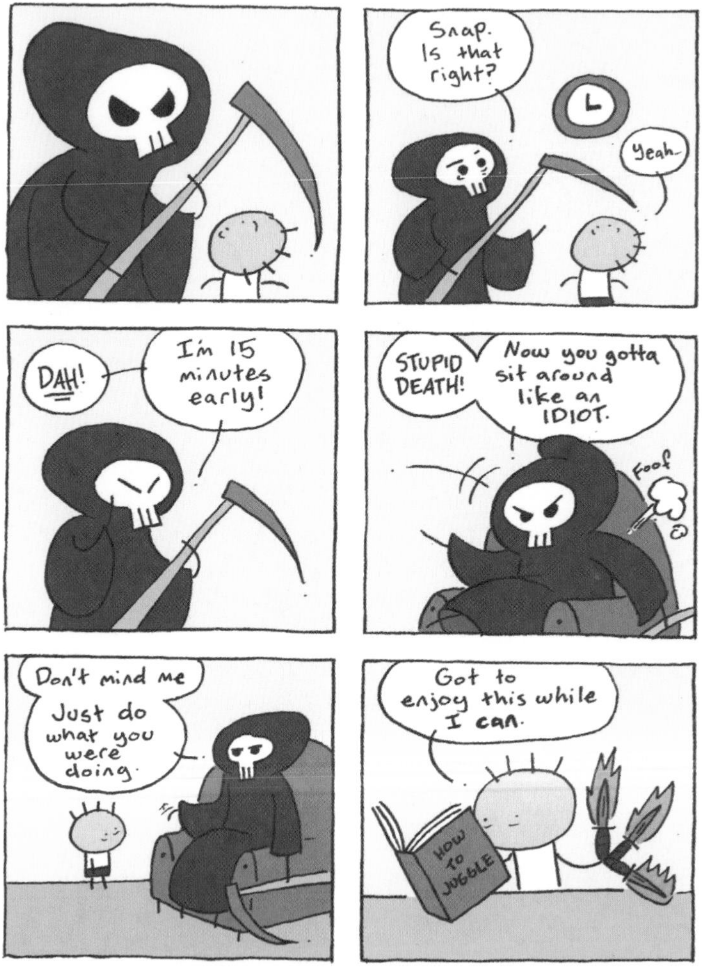

Snap.
Is that right?
Yeah.
DAH!
I'm 15 minutes early!
STUPID DEATH!
Now you gotta sit around like an IDIOT.
Foof
Don't mind me
Just do what you were doing.
Got to enjoy this while I can.
HOW TO JUGGLE

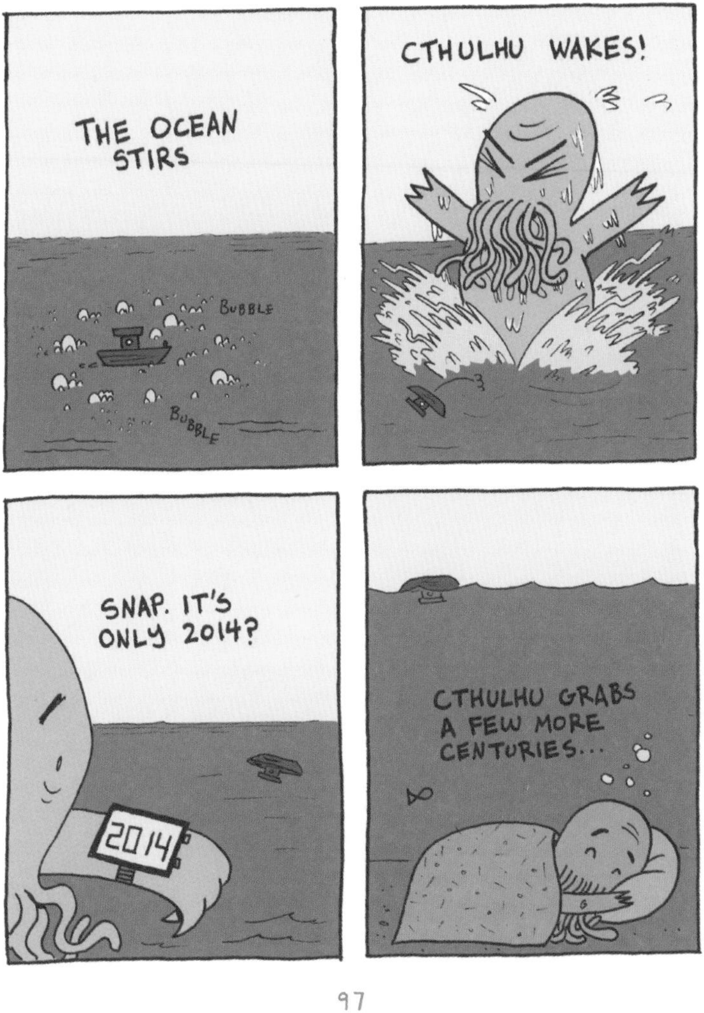
THE OCEAN STIRS
BUBBLE
BUBBLE
CTHULHU WAKES!
SNAP. IT'S ONLY 2014?
2014
CTHULHU GRABS A FEW MORE CENTURIES...

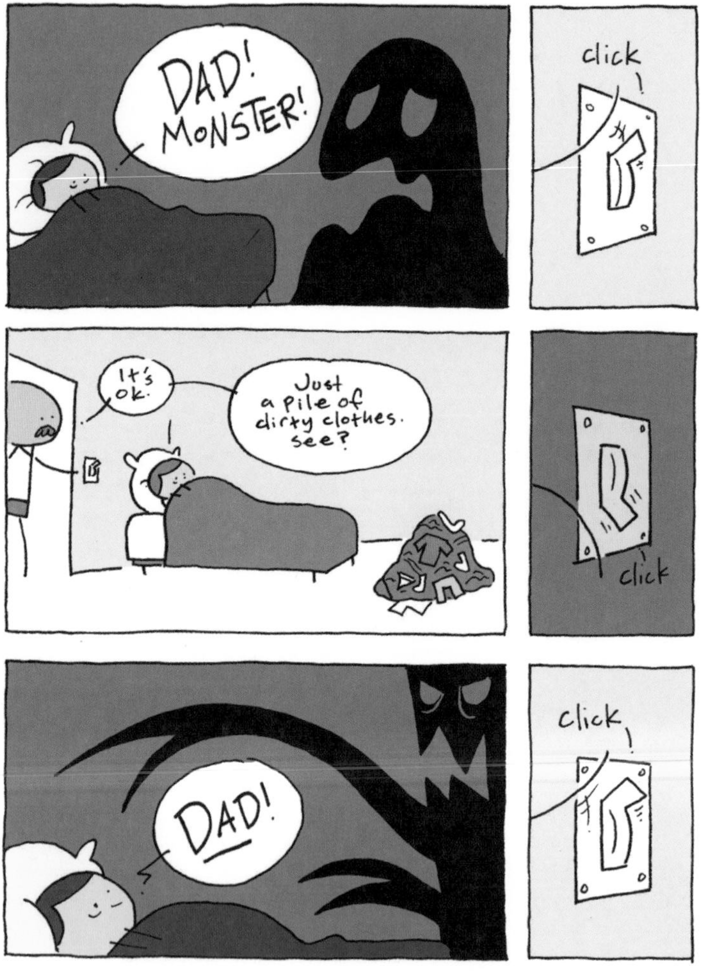
DAD! MONSTER!
click
It's ok.
Just a pile of dirty clothes. see?
click
DAD!
click

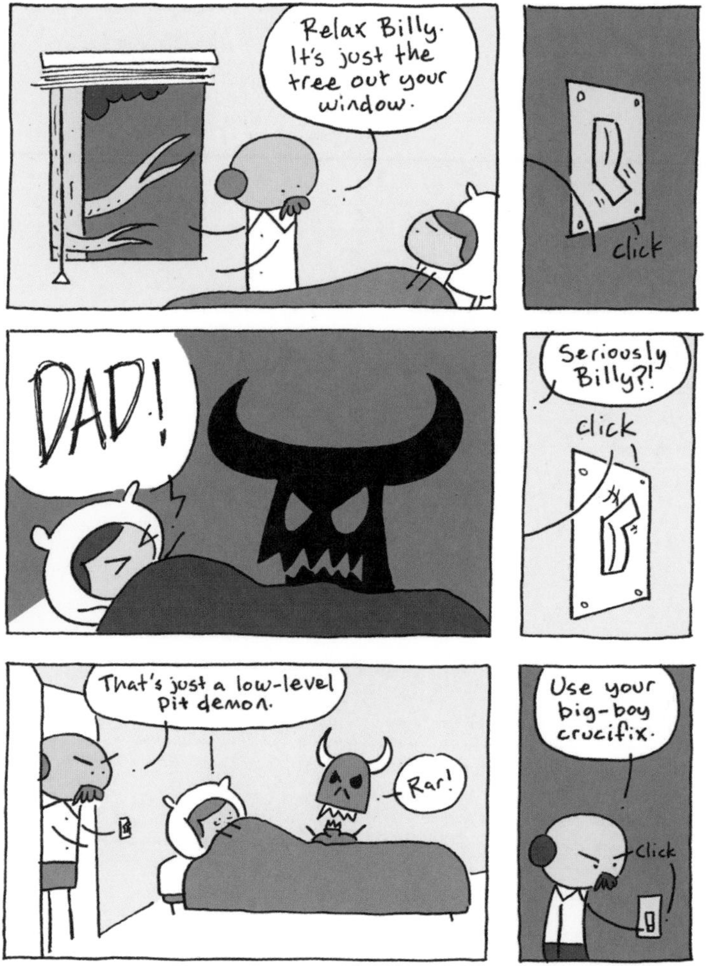
Relax Billy. It's just the tree out your window.
click
DAD!
Seriously Billy?!
click
That's just a low-level pit demon.
Rar!
Use your big-boy crucifix.
click

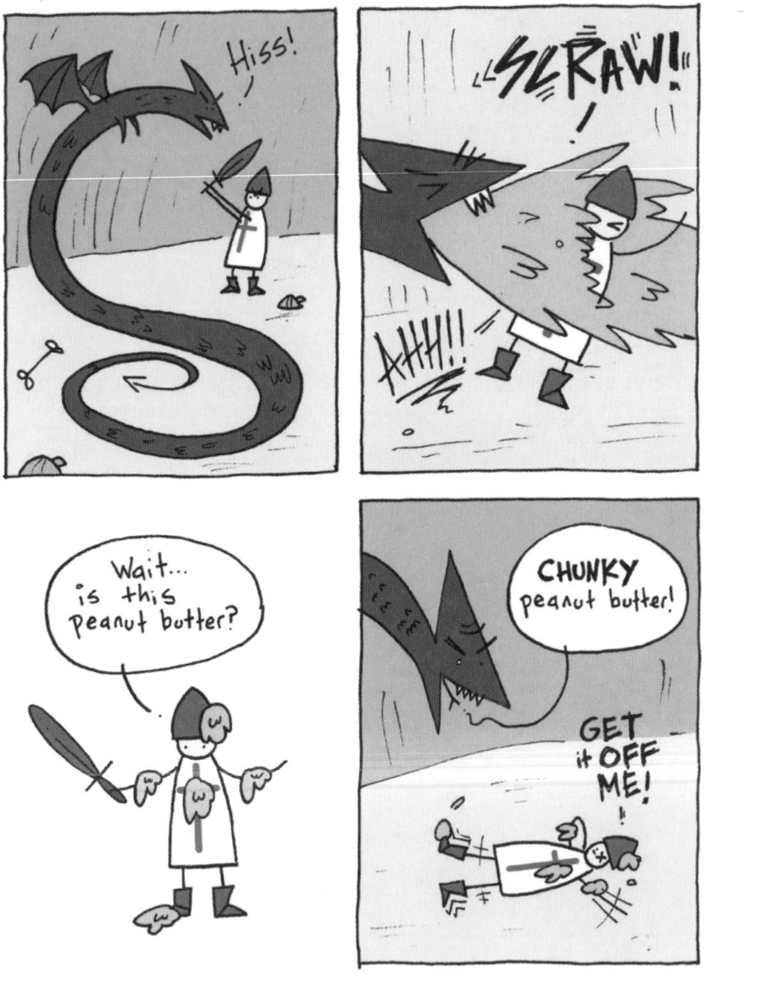
Hiss!
SCRAW!
AHH!!
Wait... is this peanut butter?
CHUNKY peanut butter!
GET it OFF ME!

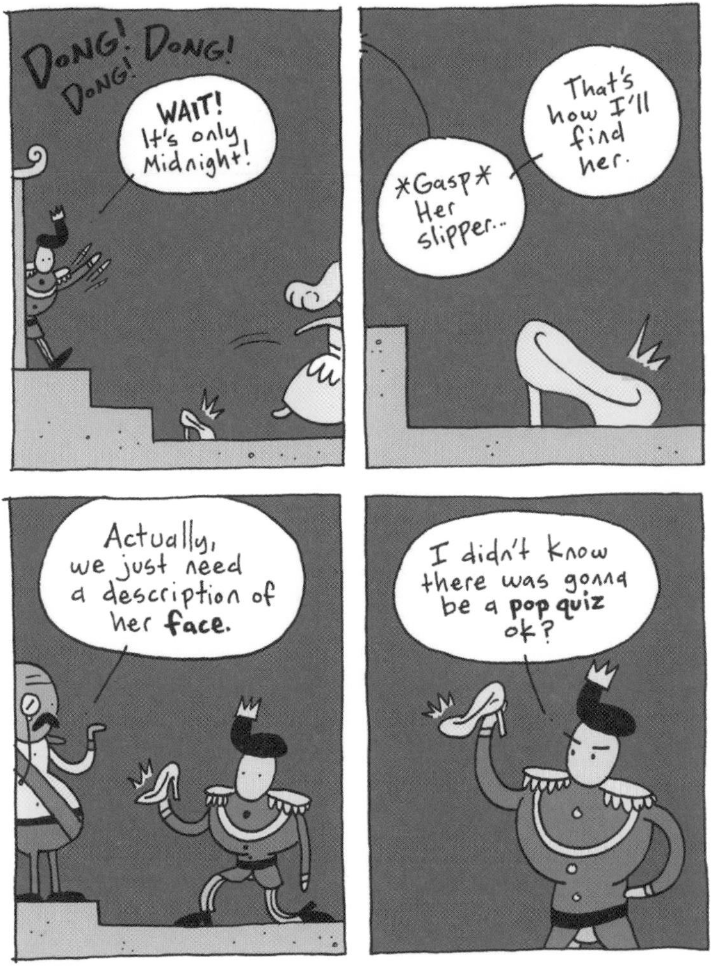
DONG! DONG! DONG!
WAIT! It's only Midnight!
Gasp Her slipper...
That's how I'll find her.
Actually, we just need a description of her face.
I didn't know there was gonna be a pop quiz ok?

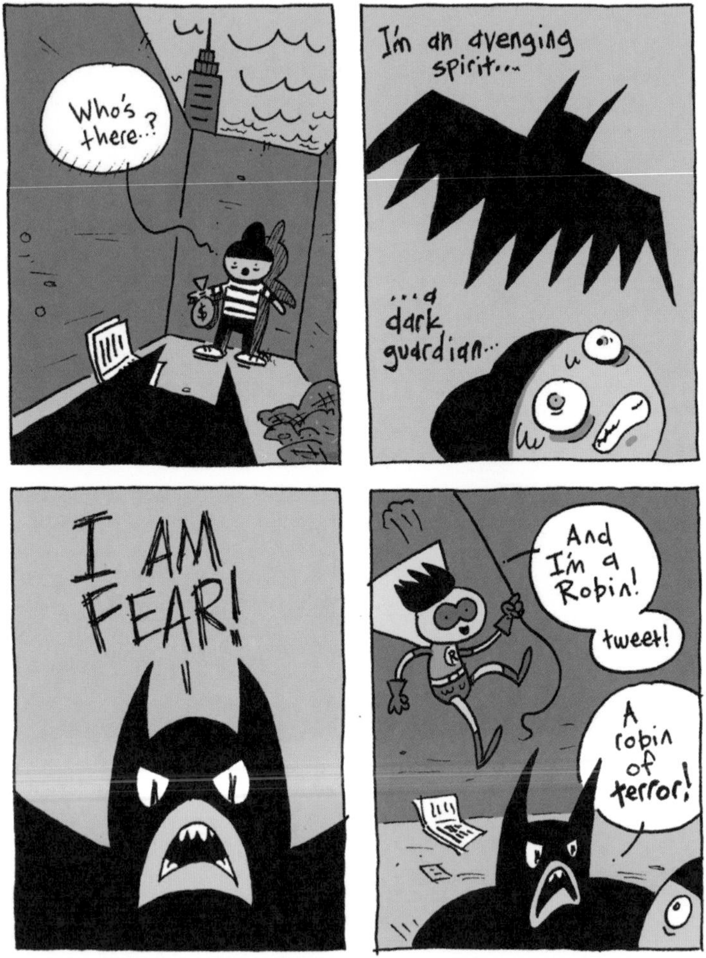
Who's there..?
I'm an avenging spirit...
...a dark guardian...
I AM FEAR!
And I'm a Robin!
tweet!
A robin of terror!

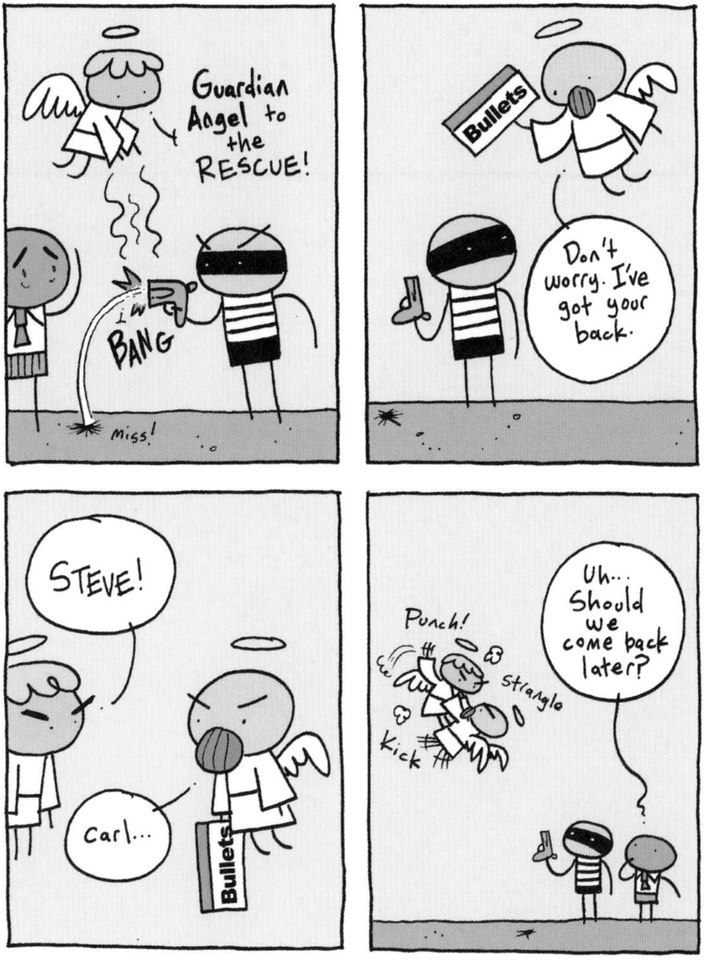
Guardian Angel to the RESCUE!
BANG
Miss!
Bullets
Don't worry. I've got your back.
STEVE!
Carl...
Bullets
Punch!
Strangle
Kick
Uh... Should we come back later?

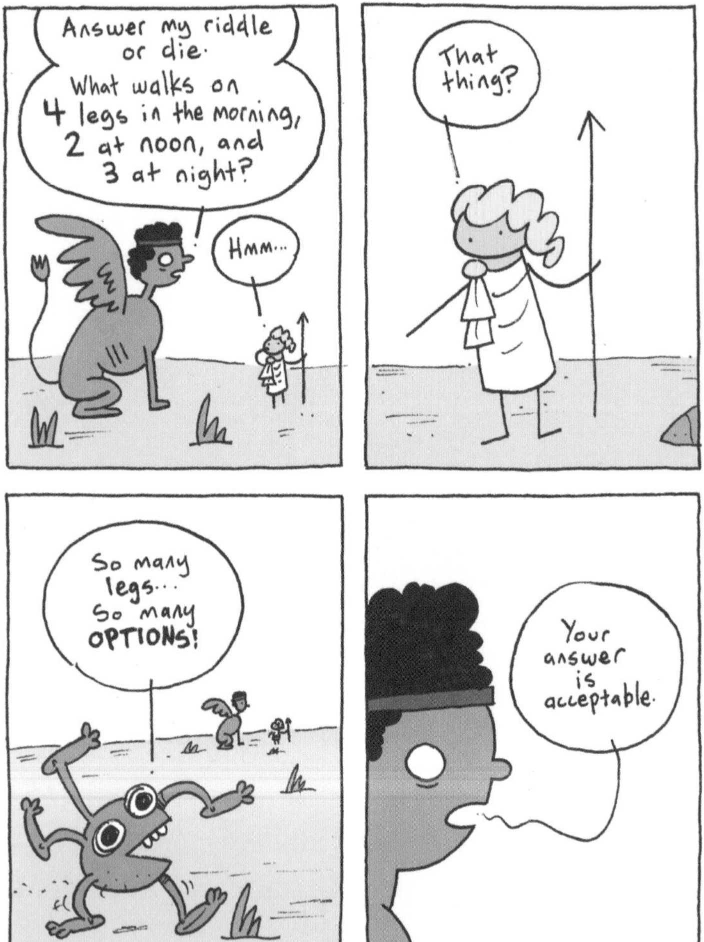
Answer my riddle or die.
What walks on 4 legs in the morning, 2 at noon, and 3 at night?
Hmm...
That thing?
So many legs... So many OPTIONS!
Your answer is acceptable.

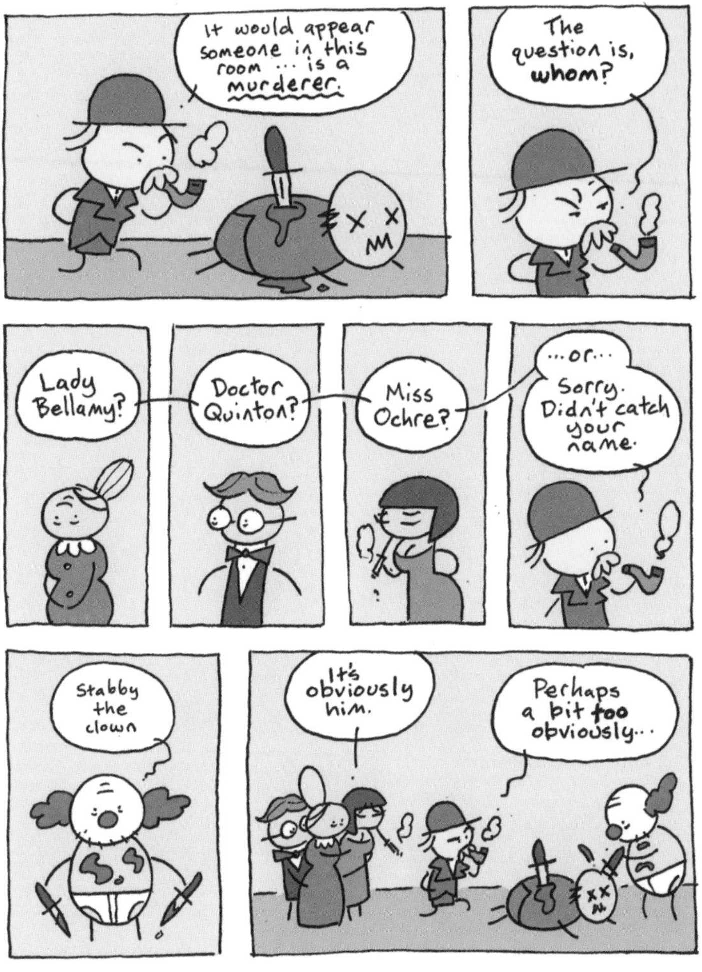
It would appear someone in this room ... is a murderer.
The question is, whom?
Lady Bellamy?
Doctor Quinton?
Miss Ochre?
...or...
Sorry. Didn't catch your name.
Stabby the clown
It's obviously him.
Perhaps a bit too obviously...

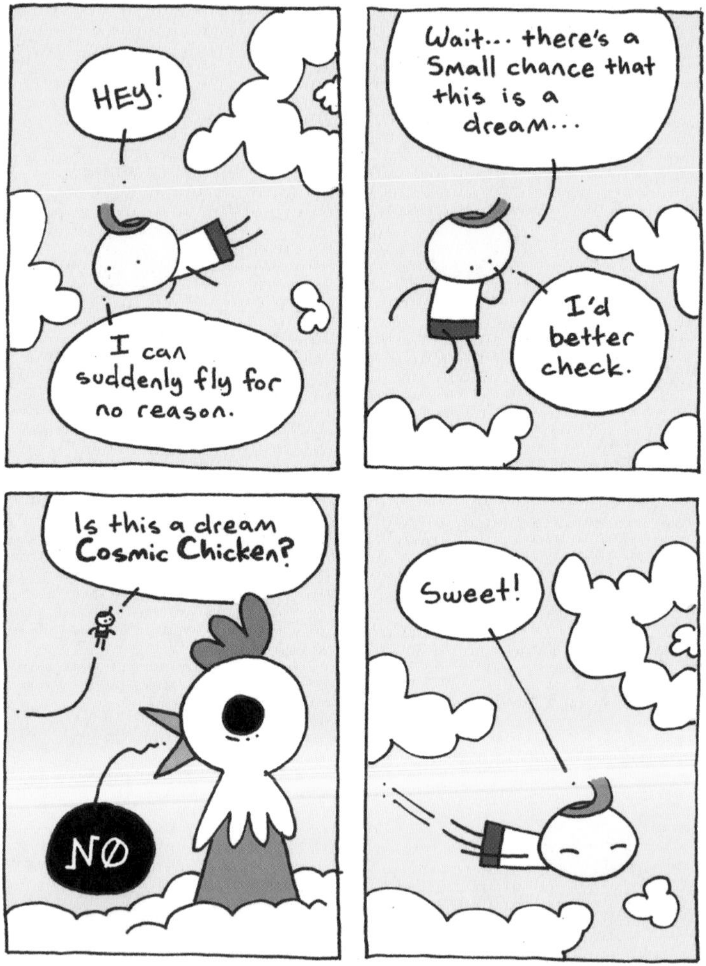
HEY!
I can suddenly fly for no reason.
Wait... there's a Small chance that this is a dream...
I'd better check.
Is this a dream Cosmic Chicken?
NØ
Sweet!

Every Zombie Scenario

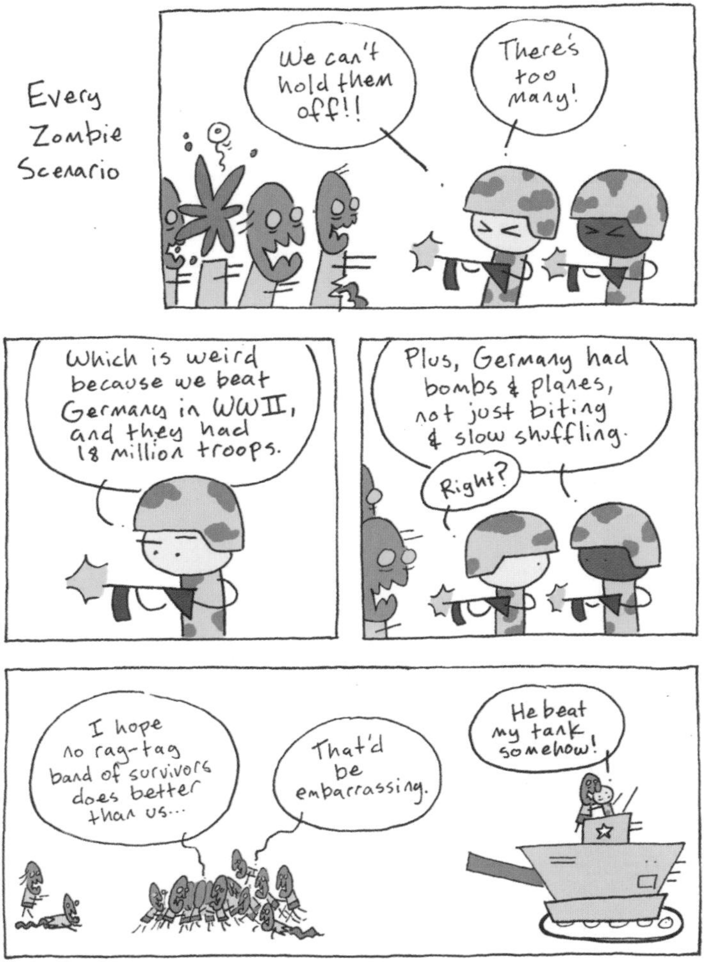

We can't hold them off!!
There's too many!
Which is weird because we beat Germany in WW II, and they had 18 million troops.
Plus, Germany had bombs & planes, not just biting & slow shuffling.
Right?
I hope no rag-tag band of survivors does better than us...
That'd be embarrassing.
He beat my tank somehow!

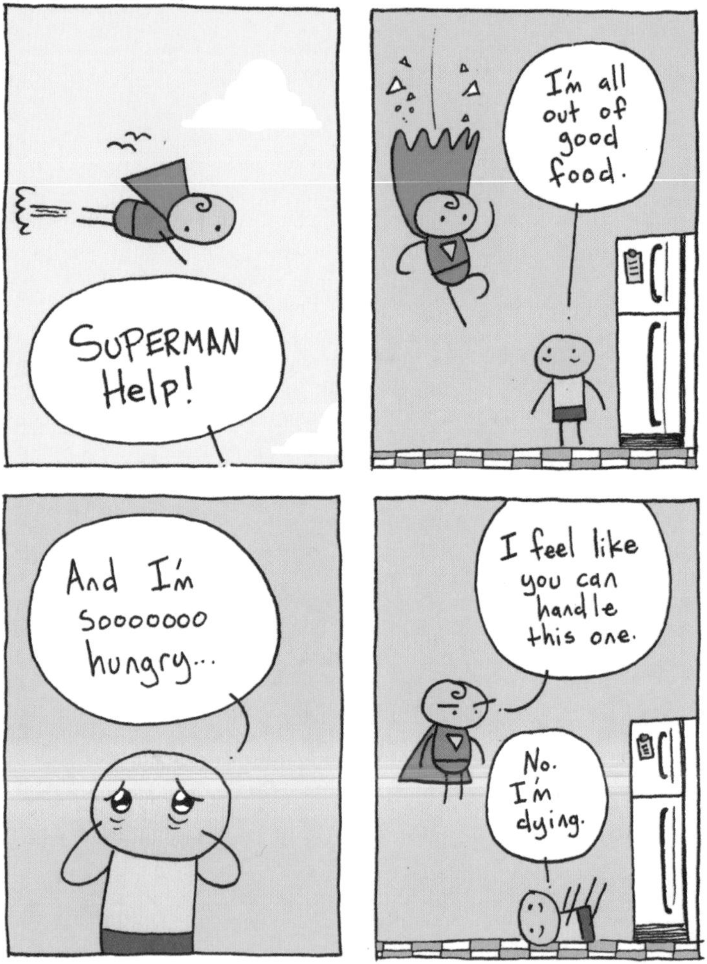
SUPERMAN Help!
I'm all out of good food.
And I'm soooooo hungry...
I feel like you can handle this one.
No. I'm dying.

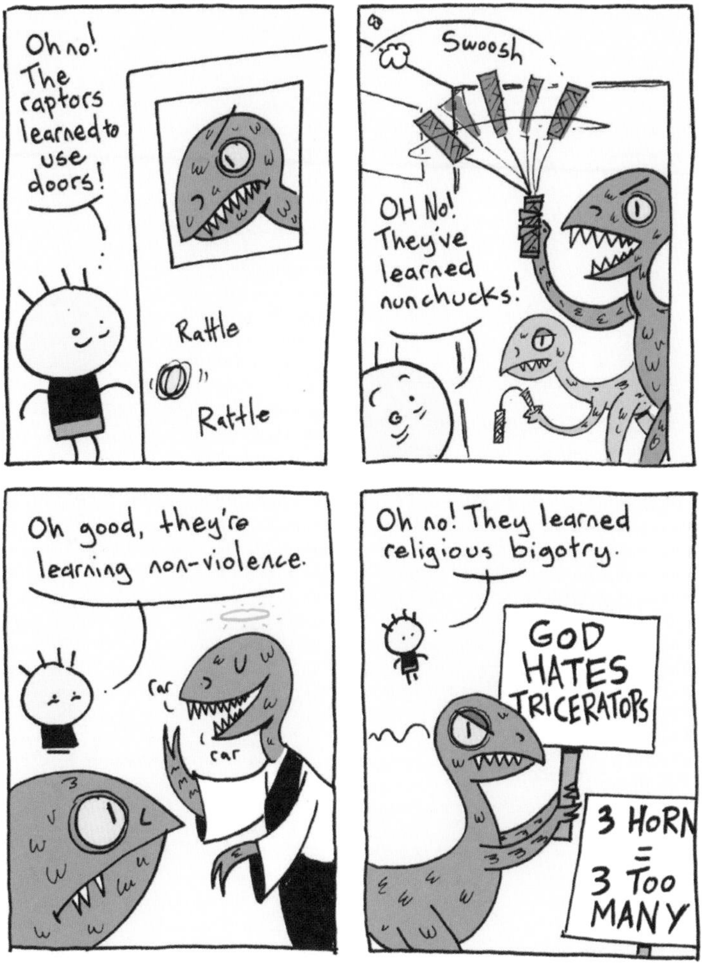
Oh no! The raptors learned to use doors!
Rattle
Rattle
Swoosh
OH No! They've learned nunchucks!
Oh good, they're learning non-violence.
rar
rar
Oh no! They learned religious bigotry.
GOD HATES TRICERATOPS
3 HORN = 3 TOO MANY

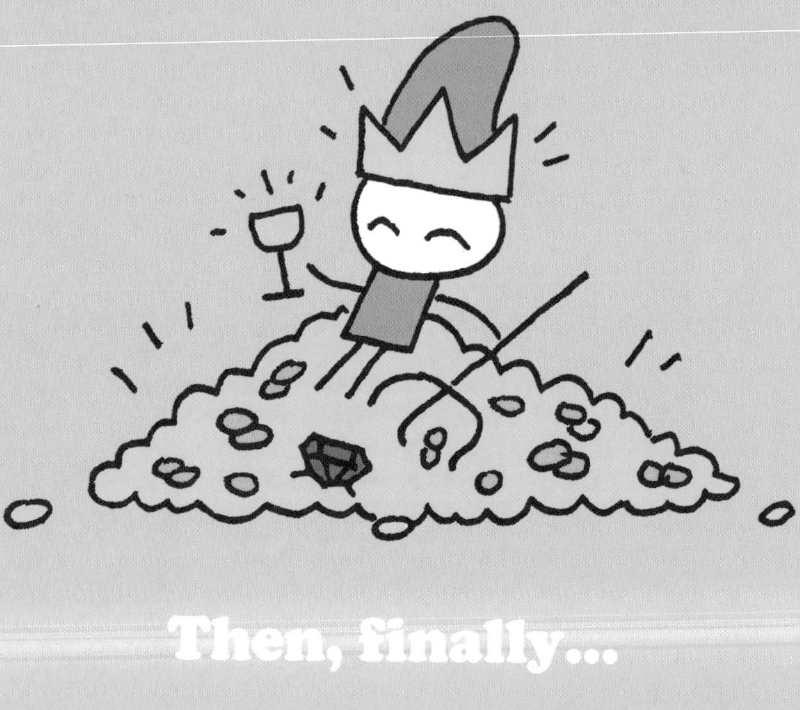

Then, finally...

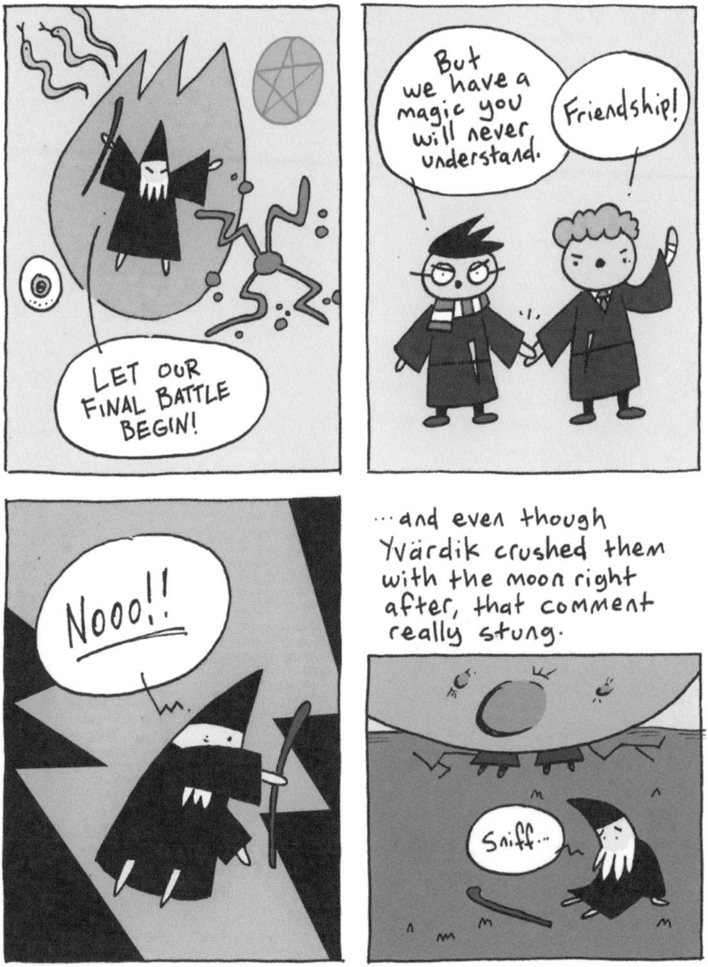
LET OUR FINAL BATTLE BEGIN!
But we have a magic you will never understand.
Friendship!
Nooo!!
...and even though Yvärdik crushed them with the moon right after, that comment really stung.
Sniff...

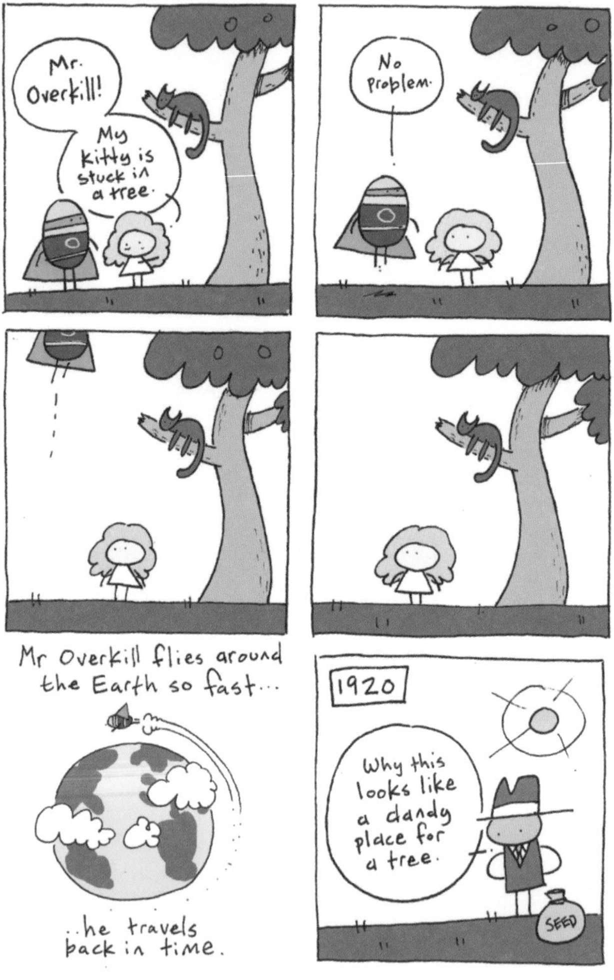
Mr. Overkill!
My kitty is stuck in a tree.
No problem.
Mr Overkill flies around the Earth so fast...
..he travels back in time.
1920
Why this looks like a dandy place for a tree.
SEED

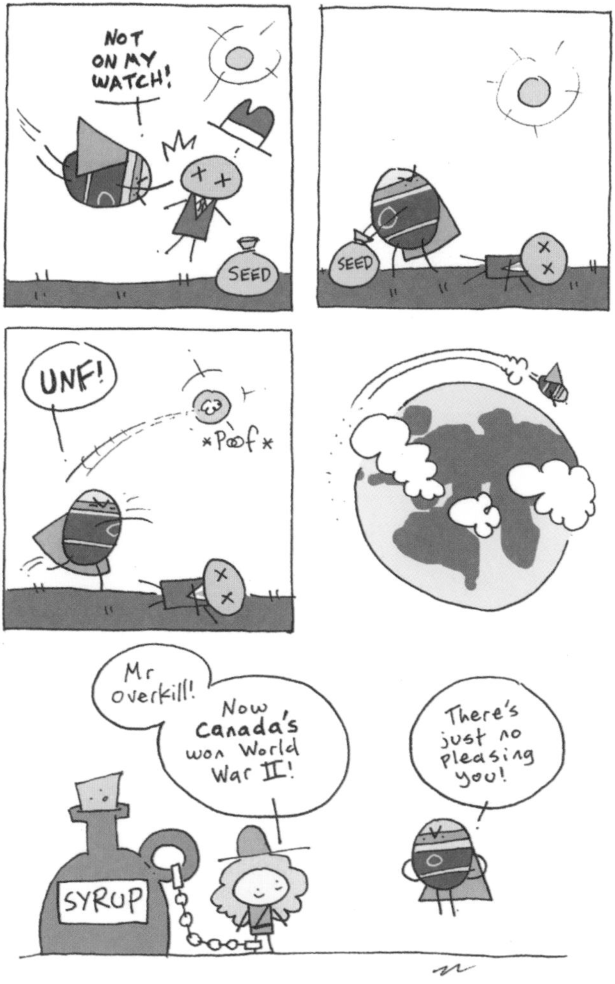
NOT ON MY WATCH!
SEED
SEED
UNF!
Poof
Mr overkill!
Now Canada's won World War II!
There's just no pleasing you!
SYRUP

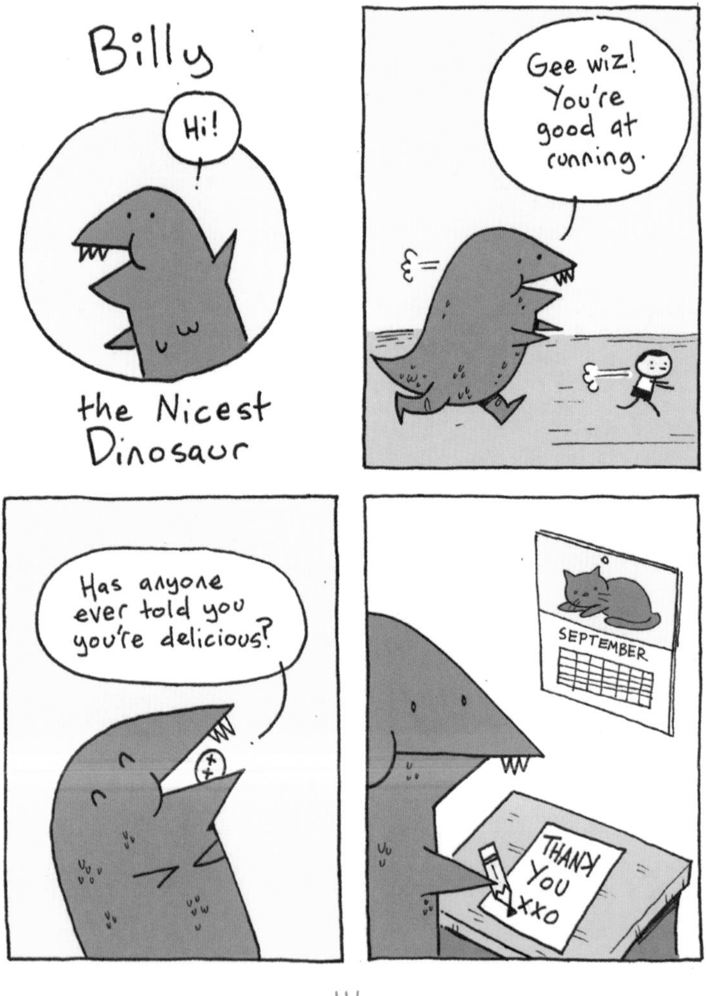
Billy
Hi!
the Nicest Dinosaur
Gee wiz! You're good at running.
Has anyone ever told you you're delicious?
SEPTEMBER
THANK YOU XXO

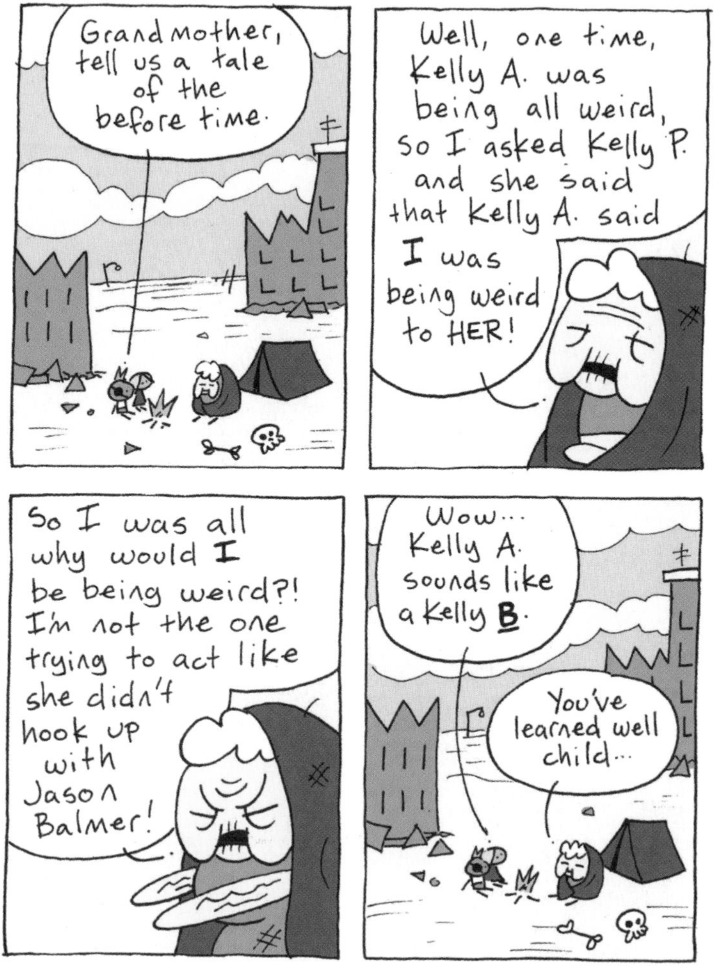
Grandmother, tell us a tale of the before time.
Well, one time, Kelly A. was being all weird, so I asked Kelly P. and she said that Kelly A. said I was being weird to HER!
So I was all why would I be being weird?! I'm not the one trying to act like she didn't hook up with Jason Balmer!
Wow... Kelly A. sounds like a Kelly B.
You've learned well child...

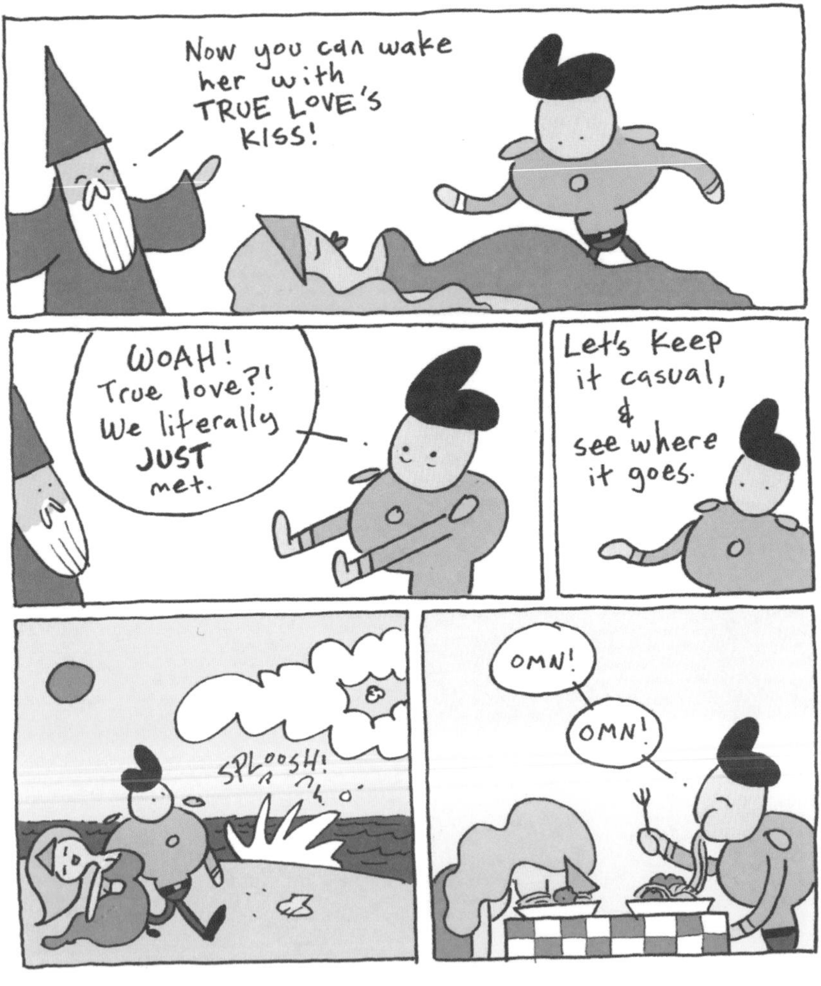
Now you can wake her with TRUE LOVE'S KISS!
WOAH! True love?! We literally JUST met.
Let's keep it casual, & see where it goes.
SPLOOSH!
OMN!
OMN!

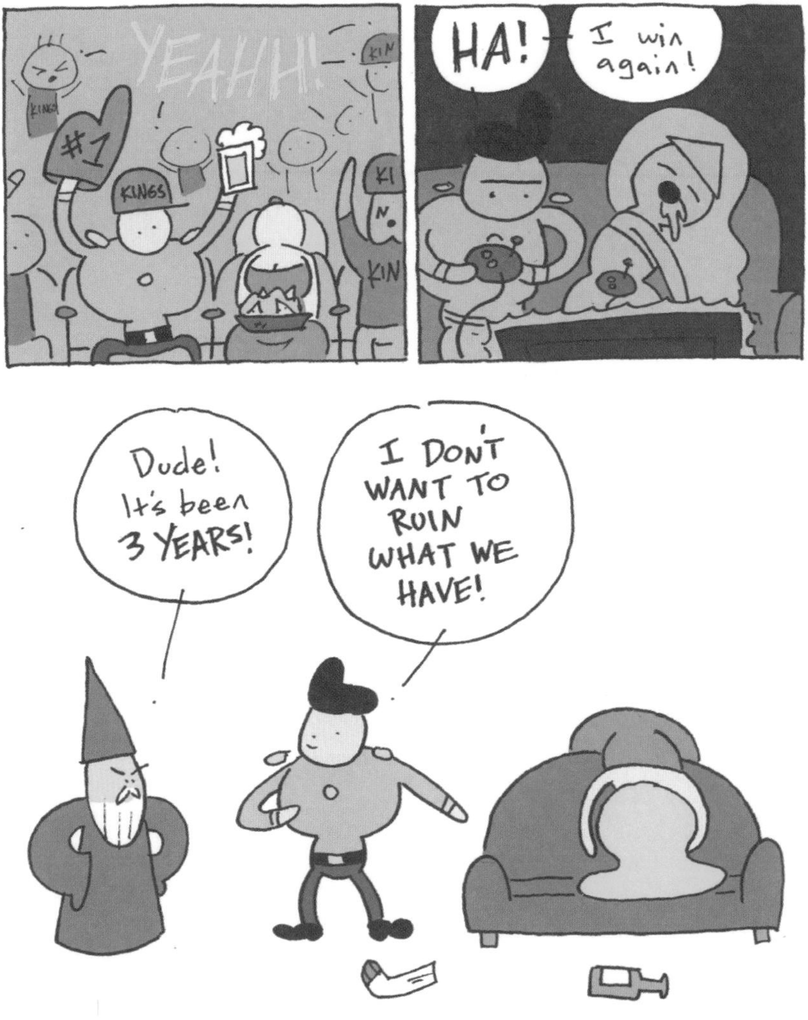
YEAHH!
#1
KINGS
HA!
I win again!
Dude! It's been 3 YEARS!
I DON'T WANT TO RUIN WHAT WE HAVE!

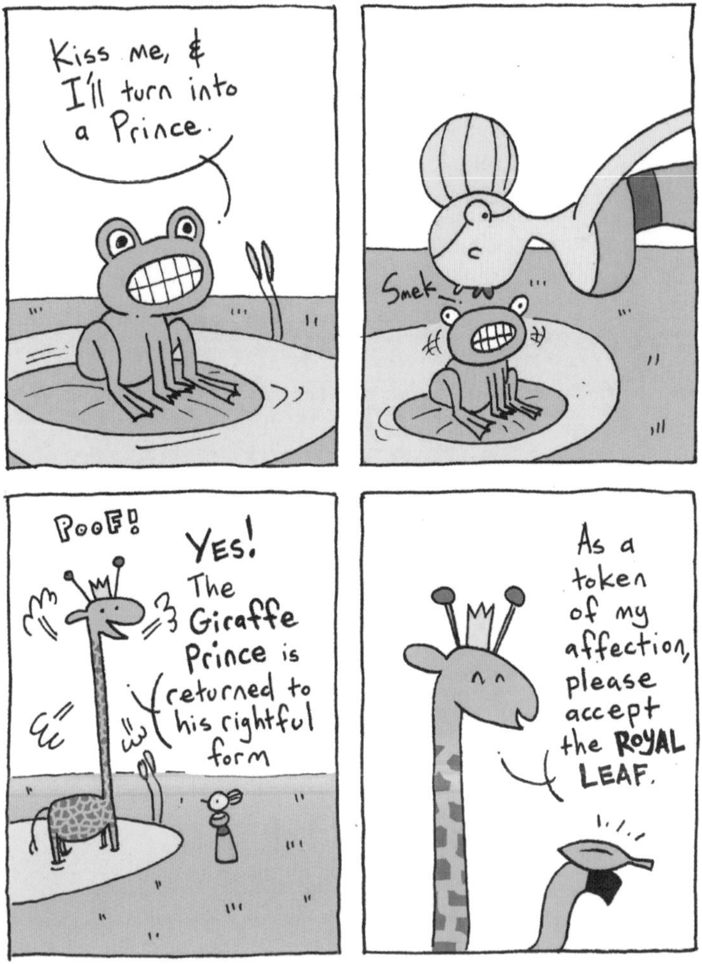
Kiss me, & I'll turn into a Prince.
Smek
POOF!
YES! The Giraffe Prince is returned to his rightful form
As a token of my affection, please accept the ROYAL LEAF.

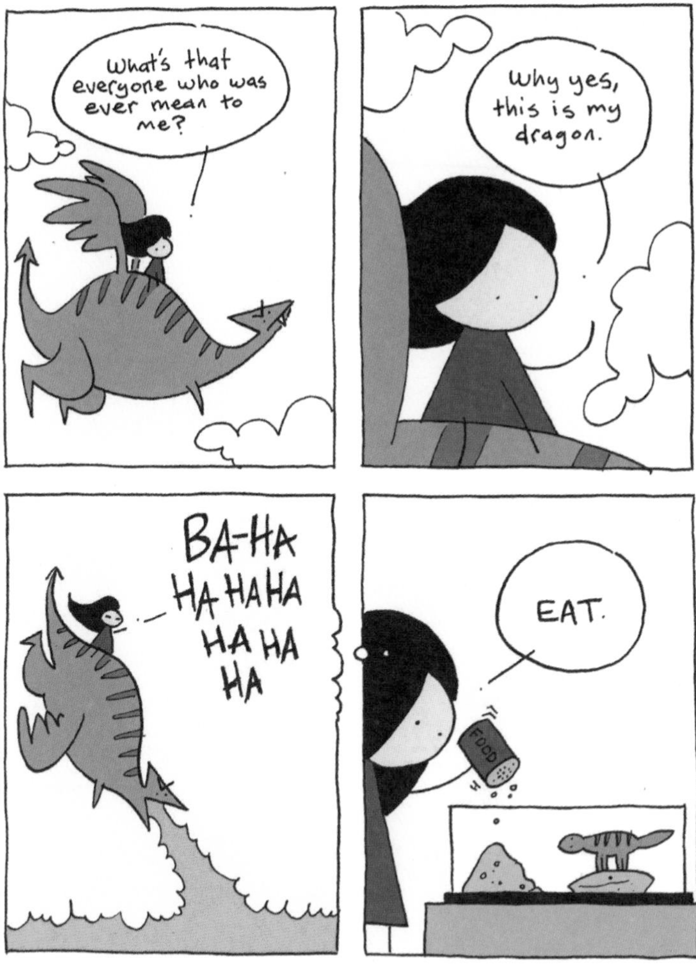
What's that everyone who was ever mean to me?
Why yes, this is my dragon.
BA-HA HA HAHA HA HA HA
EAT.
FOOD

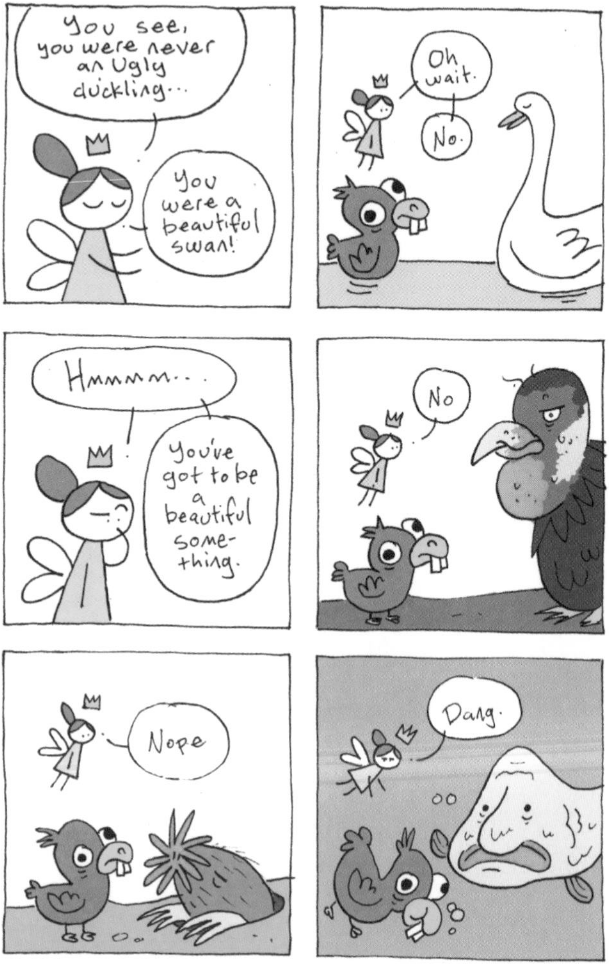
You see, you were never an Ugly duckling...
You were a beautiful swan!
Oh wait.
No.
Hmmmm...
You've got to be a beautiful some-thing.
No
Nope
Dang.

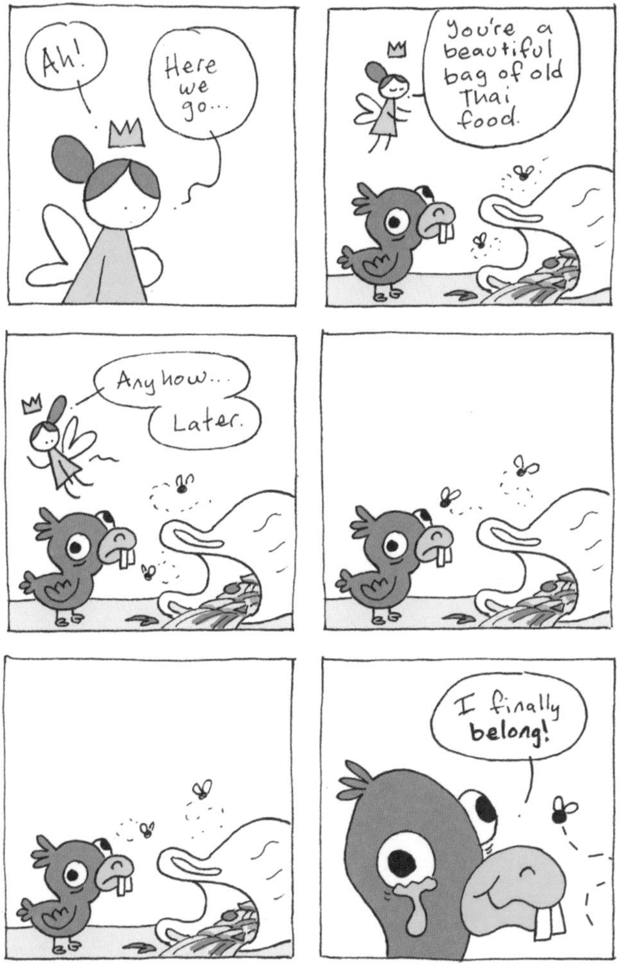
Ah!
Here we go...
You're a beautiful bag of old Thai food.
Anyhow...
Later.
I finally belong!

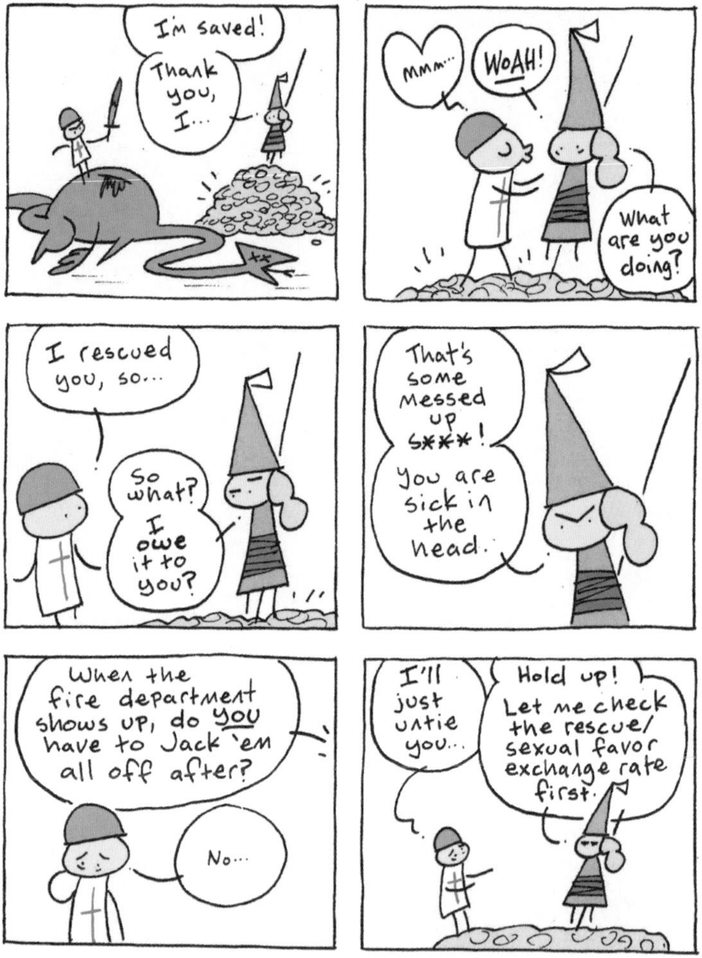
I'm saved!
Thank you, I...
MMM...
WoAH!
What are you doing?
I rescued you, so...
So what? I owe it to you?
That's some messed up S***! You are sick in the head.
When the fire department shows up, do YOU have to Jack 'em all off after?
No...
I'll just untie you...
Hold up! Let me check the rescue/sexual favor exchange rate first.

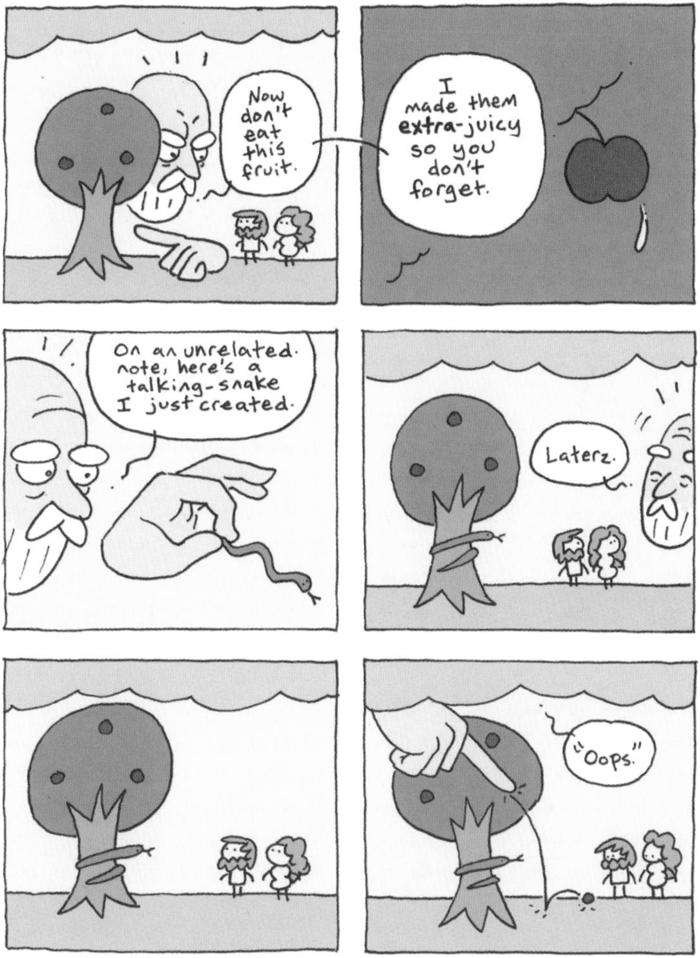
Now don't eat this fruit.
I made them extra-juicy so you don't forget.
On an unrelated note, here's a talking-snake I just created.
Laterz.
"Oops."

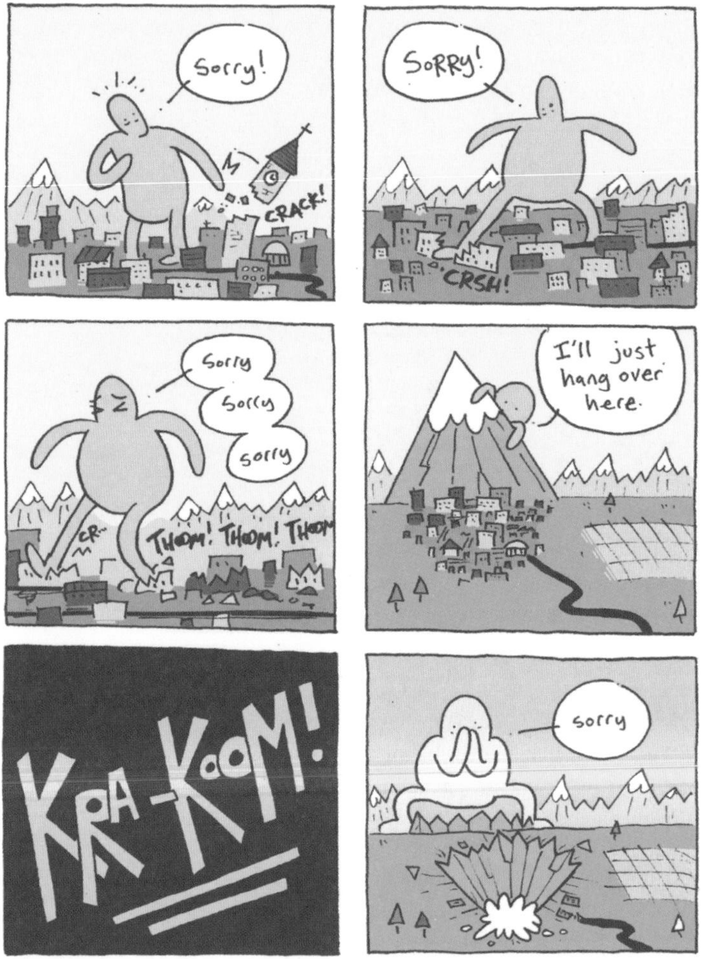
Sorry!
CRACK!
SORRY!
CRSH!
Sorry
Sorry
sorry
CR~
THOOM! THOOM! THOOM
I'll just hang over here.
KRA-KOOM!
sorry

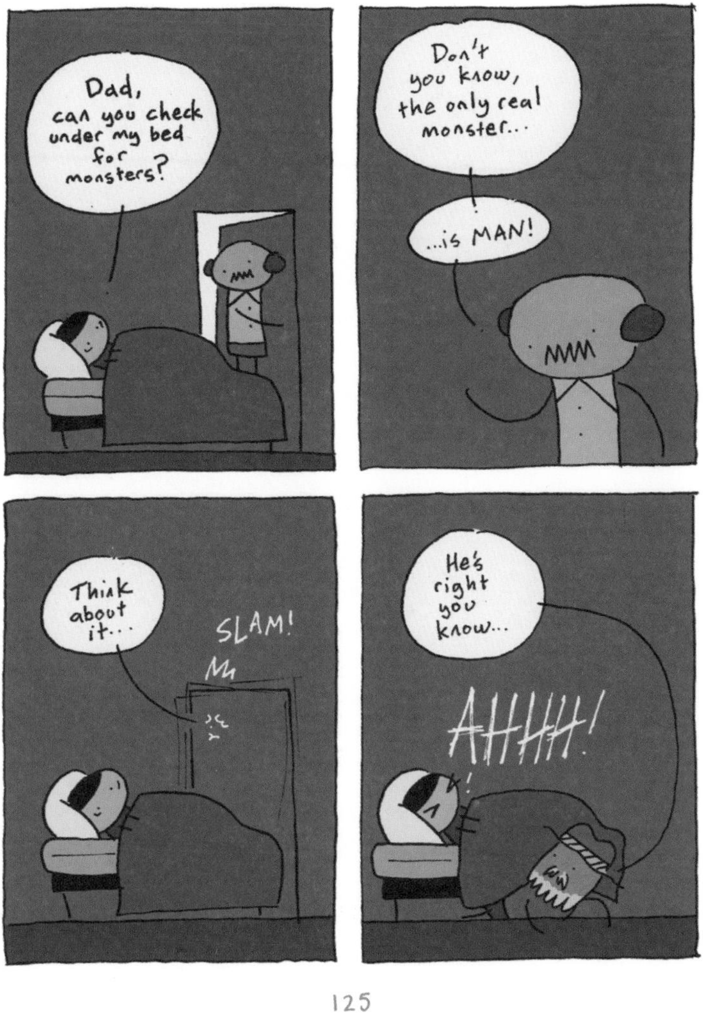
Dad, can you check under my bed for monsters?
Don't you know, the only real monster...
...is MAN!
Think about it...
SLAM!
He's right you know...
AHHH!

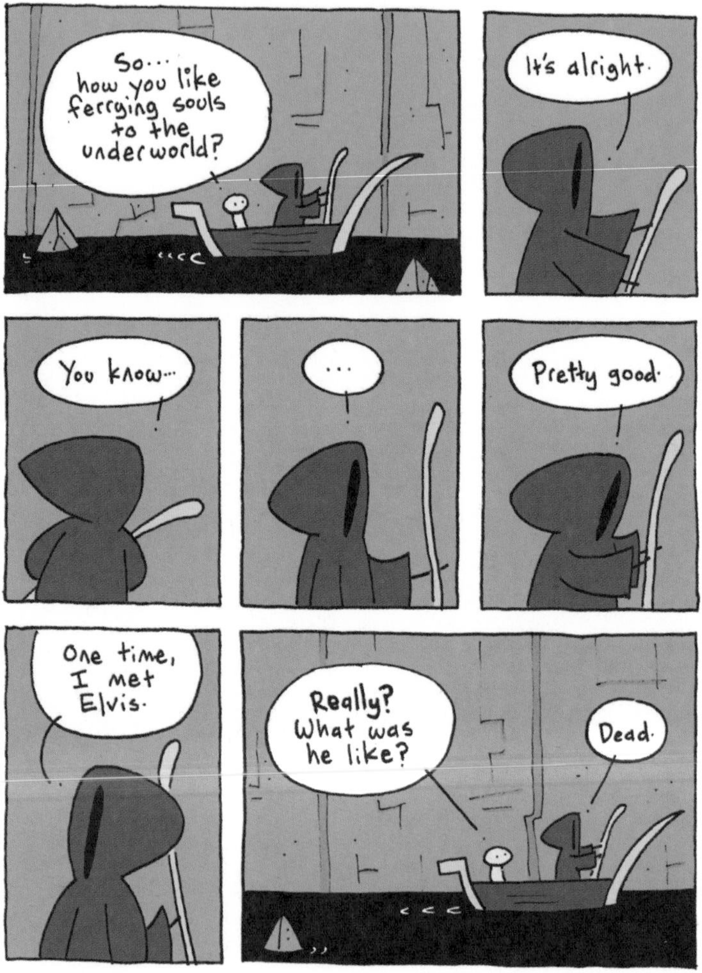
So... how you like ferrying souls to the underworld?
It's alright.
You know...
...
Pretty good.
One time, I met Elvis.
Really? What was he like?
Dead.

The end.

ISBN: 978-1-941302-57-6

Library of Congress Control Number: 2018931358

10 9 8 7 6 5 4 3 2 1